ACCLAIM FOR
Fulfilling the King's M

In *Fulfilling the King's Mission,* Dr. Betty Nwabineli unveils a solid path to the maximized life—one she continues to tread herself—a life of *excellence with an agenda.* The welding of excellence to our King and His kingdom mission—in personal life, family, career, business, and other areas of endeavour—is the hallmark of this book. She shares principles from Scripture, proven in her own life, and the wisdom of others, to help the reader apply the book. The reader will discover how to maximize their potential, the priority of family and the five-generation rule; how to invest in people, defeat odds, and use her platform in the marketplace to advance God's kingdom.

Reading it will build your capacity; by applying it, you will become, in Dr. Nwabineli's own words, a woman who is "complete in all dimensions—social, physical, mental, and spiritual . . . an excellent wife, mother, entrepreneur, and a marketplace minister." I highly recommend it!

DR. FERDINAND NWEKE
General Coordinator, Eternity Ministries
Africa Coordinator, Global Great Commission Network
Abuja, NIGERIA

This book delves into matters at the core of our faith in Jesus Christ. It helps us understand who we are from God's perspective so that purpose need not be an experiment. The experiment has already been tried by those before us; men like Solomon who, after a hedonistic spout, concluded: "Fear God!"

Dr. Betty Nwabineli gives us goalposts and not just exhortations. Every word in this book is a God-breathed blueprint for the modern woman to navigate an ever-evolving world and maintain a strong conviction whilst doing so. I have known the author for many years. Some might say she knew me whilst I was knee high to a grasshopper. Her prayers for me are reflected in the fruit of my prophetic ministry to the world. Dr. Betty is not a woman you want to learn long-distance discipleship from, and her book is an invitation card to pockets of her life, giving insight into what fulfilling the King's mission looks like in the everyday hustle and bustle of life.

I recommend this book for those whose standard has been perfectionism—it is time to change the standard to excellence! One, where you go from working for approval to working from approval. I strongly recommend this book and I am pleased to endorse its author.

PROPHET/APOSTLE TOMI ARAYOMI
Founder of RIG Nation & Managing Director of Prophetic Voice TV
Windsor, United Kingdom

Dr. Betty Nwabineli has written this book to inspire women to live a Christian life of excellence. It will prove valuable for men who desire to live excellently and support their partners to excel. The book will benefit every reader. It draws from the author's life, particularly her wealth of experience as a wife, mother and grandmother.

A very well-researched book that draws from various authors, across ancient classics to the contemporary. It is a rich resource, helpful to any serious-minded person who desires to live a life of value. Well-presented and easy to follow, in many parts, it is as if the writer is conversing with the reader with straight talk where required. I could not help but smile, when I read, "Oh, I know there are some bossy wives, but if their husbands don't know how to take care of them, let them go ahead and be henpecked." The flow from her thoughts to relevant and helpful Scriptures and back is smooth. The logic and reasoning are engaging, well founded, and accommodating to people of all backgrounds.

A non-fictional book that is truly spiritually encouraging and enriching, Dr. Betty Nwabineli talks about how she came into an authentic relationship with God. She also shares her life's experiences and testimonies of God's faithfulness. She reflects on God's blessings on her life and describes how holding on to God helped through challenging times. By patience and commitment to excellence in God, she achieved feats that would have caused others to succumb and live a life of gloom and dejection. It is helpful that she attributes her successes to the grace of God, while of course accompanying her faith with works.

The book draws from a life of service and commitment to support others to live a fulfilled life of excellence in God. It is worth hearty commendation to every believer, regardless of gender or age. Happy reading!

PROFESSOR JOHN DURODOLA
Head of Mechanical Engineering. Oxford Brookes University,
Oxford, United Kingdom

As an organisational psychologist, I have spent a lifetime encouraging organisations to start their journey to greatness. Invariably, the key to leaders being sufficiently motivated to change hinges on a visible example of a great, virtuous organisation-the type they can aspire to become.

Applying this motivational principle, what better encouragement to live a life of excellence, than reading this incredible book?

As the reader digests each chapter, I am confident that it will inspire them to apply its biblical principles for living a life of excellence.

There is evidence in each page and her life's story that Dr. Betty Nwabineli has a genuine passion for and complete grasp of her subject. And so, can *talk the talk*. Also, it is evident that she is well along on her journey of *living the life of excellence*, that God intended for her as a purposeful individual, wife, mother, grandmother and marketplace minister. Thus, she can also *walk the walk*!

On a professional level, I recommend this book to all male and female managers, leaders, business owners, and coaches to business leaders. It is full of proven and practical insights, methods and approaches that have made the author a very effective leader, business owner, and highly respected woman of God.

HONOURABLE JIM COWAN
Chairperson, Value the Person International
Durham, United Kingdom

Whatever you read in this book you will find embodied in Dr. Betty Nwabineli and her husband Dr. James Nwabineli. We have known this family for over twenty-five years, and they are unwavering in their faith and zeal for following Jesus. They, as a couple, carry a *most excellent* spirit which is evident within minutes of meeting them.

Betty has achieved much in her career, business ventures and Christian faith. She adds her voice, with biblical and academic authority and depth of personal experience, to inspire us to excel through the power of the Holy Spirit in every area of our lives. Be prepared to be inspired and challenged. If we embrace the truths in this book, our lives will change. We will accomplish much for His kingdom in our lives, in the lives of those we love and the next generation.

PASTORS GLYN AND JEAN CARTER
Marketplace Ministers, Kingdom Culture Church
Spennymoor, United Kingdom

It is with great pleasure and excitement that I take this opportunity to review this book. The author, known to me for many years, has epitomised the Proverbs 31 woman. Her dedication, commitment, and love for the body of Christ is highly visible. She is contagious in her endeavour to walk the life of faith, to live and to love as Jesus taught us. Dr. Betty is instrumental in raising women of character, confidence, and consistency in the things of God.

This book will inform, reform, and transform our thinking of who we are and how we can live a life pleasing to our Maker. Dr. Betty Nwabineli is used of God as a signpost to guide women into their destiny and fulfil their God-given purpose.

I highly recommend this book. It is not a soft touch for people on milk; it is a banquet of rich, healthy food. It will benefit those who are committed to pressing towards the mark of the highest calling in Christ Jesus. It may require chewing longer, but the benefits will be great. As you move through the pages, you will discover fresh revelations of the King of kings. You will also be able to test the depths of your faith, the height of your confidence and the quality of your actions. Not only that, but many will recover their balance and strive forward with new enthusiasm and renewed power.

God has raised up my sister for such a time as this, to be a voice to the nations. Men and women will benefit from reading this book. The reward will be that we have a balanced view of serving our King. The knowledge and insight we gain will be invaluable for our future. Whatever our position in life, we will be challenged to go deeper in God and become God's masterpieces in this generation.

REV. JOYCELYN VASSEL
Overseer—Shammah International Ministries
Milton-Keynes, United Kingdom

Many strive to stand out in a crowd. However, very few leave lasting impressions worthy of emulation. Fashion, flair, fame, and fortune do not necessarily promote the right image. This book emblazes personified excellence! Dr. Betty Nwabineli's reflective practice is a masterpiece carved out of cherished childhood, life choices, lifestyle and calling. The narratives benefit from the legacy of positive parenting received and nurtured. Her appetite for godly wisdom scripted in the Bible as well as historical and contemporary literature; and daily dosage of excellence woven into her tapestry of domestic, professional, vocational and kingdom living accredit her for the daunting task of writing her autograph!

This book is an invitation to a lifelong adventure in excellence, a path less travelled. Dr. Betty Nwabineli does not just commend the reader to the grace of excellence, but she charges the reader to "go and do likewise!"

I commend this book to all, male, or female, young or elderly. The read is easy, but lessons priceless! I hope that it will be translated to many languages as excellence is culture neutral! It has been an honour to read the book.

PASTOR (MRS) DUPE ADEFALA
Word Fountain Christian Ministries
Cowley—Oxford, United Kingdom

Jesus was noticeably clear in his instructions on how we would know mature, faithful Christians. Dr. Betty Nwabineli, you stand as a woman of God in leadership; a shining example to us all. You have lived a transparent life, taught us the Word of God in speech, by example and in role play, practicing what you preach, focused on knowing God and pleasing Him, and bearing the fruit of the Spirit, in all humility.

Thank you for sharing the truth with us. All who read this book will gain a rich inheritance that has been delivered to us through love, perseverance, suffering and endurance. We are truly blessed for knowing you.

BISHOP DR. SUZANNE NTI
Chief Operating Officer, Action Chapel International Worldwide
VP Nicholas Duncan-Williams Ministries, Provost NDW School of Ministry
Accra, Ghana

Dr. Betty Nwabineli is a woman of grace, integrity, courage and truly a woman of excellence. However, in this book, she also commends herself as a true exponent of the Word of God bringing clarity, truth, and revelation to the reader.

A celebration of the destiny of women but pertinent also to men, you will be challenged and inspired as Dr. Betty Nwabineli expounds on her own pursuit of excellence and enthralled by the telling of her own personal story beginning in her roots in Nigeria.

This is a book which will benefit all who turn its pages–a classic for such a time as this.

PASTOR LOIS GOTT
Senior Pastor, Bethshan Church
Washington, United Kingdom

This book is a clarion call to any woman who wants to please God and serve His purpose for her generation. It is a blueprint for success for any godly woman in pursuit of fulfilling God's plan and purpose. I was struck by how much Dr. Betty Nwabineli has laid bare her core and essence in its pages. She has meticulously dealt with every aspect of the life of a woman. Readers are equipped and empowered to live the abundant life that God intends for all. This book is a well of knowledge and wisdom that many will drink from and be satisfied. As you read through, you cannot but feel the sincerity of Dr. Betty's heart as well as her desire to impact lives for Christ. The testimonies littered throughout the book will provoke you to seek and know God. Dr. Betty has not just written a book; she has left a legacy–footprints in the sand of time.

MINISTER MORIN CAREW
Founder and Director of Right Impressions Ltd,
Founder, God's Own Woman Ministries
London, United Kingdom

Dr. Betty Ivie Nwabineli stands as a pillar of excellence in the midst of so much mediocrity and wind-blown confusion that is ripping apart marriages and homes. Her commitment to integrity, womanhood, and spiritual passion is a joy to behold. She exhibited the qualities of a tender loving woman, mother, and companion right from her University days. *Fulfilling the King's Mission: A Blueprint for Kingdom Women of Excellence*, is a practical demonstration of her life story and a *must read* for every married couple desiring a successful married life. It will also make an excellent read for single men and women, boys and girls preparing for marriage. It is a 'must have' in every library, private or public.

PROFESSOR CLARA LEYIBO IGELEKE
Professor of Microbiology, Benson Idahosa University,
Benin City, Nigeria

I reiterate that in my opinion, to glorify God with our entire lives is the ultimate purpose for which everyone was created. That is the highest level of living. That gives this book the place of relevance and of course true excellence that it is conveying! Well done for a timely, relevant and powerful tapestry of beauty, experience and wisdom for our time and the next generation of women, mothers and daughters! It is a must read!!!

APOSTLE ENOMFON NTEFON
Lead—Kingdom Women in Ministry Globally
London, United Kingdom

FULFILLING THE
KING'S
MISSION

FULFILLING THE
KING'S
MISSION

A Blueprint for
Kingdom Women of Excellence

BETTY IVIE NWABINELI

Nwabineli

BE BLESSED AND EMPOWERED AS YOU READ

WEDNESDAY, 21 APRIL 2021

credo
house publishers

ISBN: 978-1-62586-194-8

Published in the United States of America by Credo House Publishers,
a division of Credo Communications LLC, Grand Rapids, Michigan
credohousepublishers.com

Cover and interior design by Klaas Wolterstorff / kwbookdesign.com

First editing by Funmilayo Joy Bafuwa (Heritage Editing Services, Washington, UK)
Final editing by Chloe Ford (Credo House Publishers, Michigan, USA)

**Scripture quotations in this book were taken from
these publications and we wish to acknowledge them:**
Scripture quotations marked ASV are from the *American Standard Version* (public domain)
Scripture quotations marked AMP are taken from the *Amplified Bible*, copyright © 1954, 1958, 1962,
1964, 1965, 1987 by The Lockman Foundation. Used by permission.
Scripture quotations marked AMPC are taken from the *Amplified Bible Classic* edition, copyright © 1954,
1958, 1962, 1964, 1965, 1987 by The Lockman Foundation Used by permission. www.Lockman.org
Scripture quotations marked CEV are from the *Contemporary English Version,* copyright © 1991, 1992,
1995 by American Bible Society. Used by Permission.
Scripture quotations marked GW are from *God's Word* translation, Christian Doctrine, Washington, D.C.
and are used by permission of the copyright owner.
Scripture quotations marked KJV are from the *King James Version* (public domain)
Scripture quotations marked NASB are taken from the *New American Standard Bible*, copyright ©
1960, 1962, 1963, 1968, 1971, 1972, 1973, 1975, 1977, 1995 by The Lockman Foundation Used by
permission. www.Lockman.org
Scripture quotations marked NIV are taken from the *Holy Bible,* New International Version, NIV.
Copyright © 1973, 1978, 1984, 2011 by Biblica, Inc. Used by permission of Zondervan. All rights
reserved worldwide.www.zondervan.com
Scripture quotations marked NKJV are taken from the *New King James Version,* copyright © 1982 by
Thomas Nelson. Used by permission. All rights reserved.
Scripture quotations marked NLT are taken from the *Holy Bible, New Living Translation,* copyright
©1996, 2004, 2015 by Tyndale House Foundation. Used by permission of Tyndale House
Publishers, a Division of Tyndale House Ministries, Carol Stream, Illinois 60188. All rights
reserved.
Scripture quotations marked MSG are taken from *The Message,* copyright © 1993, 2002, 2018 by Eugene
H. Peterson. Used by permission of NavPress Publishing Group.
Scripture quotations marked TLB are taken from *The Living Bible copyright* ©1971. Used by permission of
Tyndale House Publishers, a Division of Tyndale House Ministries, Carol Stream, Illinois 60188.
All rights reserved.
Scripture quotations marked WEB are taken from the *World English Bible* (public domain)
Scripture quotations marked WNT are taken from *The Weymouth New Testament*, otherwise known as
The New Testament in Modern Speech or The Modern Speech New Testament, is a translation of
the New Testament into nineteenth century English by Richard Francis Weymouth, edited and
partly revised by Ernest Hampden-Cook. London: James Clark and Co., 1903.
Scriptures are presented in this book as obtained from Bible different translations. In some instances,
I have added emphasis in bold. Some Scripture verses are cited without references to any
translation of the Bible, indicating non-preference for a Bible translation.

DEDICATION

This book is lovingly, passionately, and gratefully dedicated to:
The Triune GOD:

The Father (for loving me so much and sending His only begotten Son, Jesus, to die for me); The Son, Jesus Christ, my Saviour, and Intercessor, who willingly died to atone for my sin and to reconcile me to God; The Holy Spirit, my Paraclete and Teacher.
I love, adore, honour, worship, and appreciate You!

My wonderful and loving family:
Dr. Nwachukwu James, my beloved husband.
The man of my dreams and best friend for forty-three years.
Your understanding heart has been a source of strength and continual support. Thank you for your love and guiding example! Your generosity, prayers, gentle encouragement, inspiration, and good humour have made this book a reality. You make me feel special.
I love you!

Our precious, blessed, and highly favoured children and family:
Ngozichukwuka, Chukwumaobi, Onyedikachukwu, Charlene, Elijah Chukwunonsu.
You are the earthly lights of my life and inspiration.
Family is what empowers us to work out what we talk about.
You bring me more joy than I could have ever hoped for.
Being your mother/grandmother is one of my greatest earthly rewards.
My heart thanks you for your love, prayers, encouragement, and inspiration.
I bless you for your vital insights and resolute confidence in me.

To my late parents:
Elder Vincent Ebhodaghe Okoh and Madam Angelina Inegbene Okoh.
Thank you for believing in me and showing me that:
Love truly conquers all.

To all who through this book will fulfil the King's call on their lives, help to raise godly generations and believe that undeniably,
"WITH GOD, ALL THINGS ARE POSSIBLE!"

Contents

Acknowledgements

I want to start by expressing my deepest gratitude to the original Dreamer—GOD. He put the dream of writing this book in my heart. He also made it happen in His time. I am eternally grateful to You, faithful and awesome LORD!

> Yours, O Lord, is the greatness and the power and the glory and the victory and the majesty, for all that is in the heavens and the earth is Yours; Yours is the kingdom, O Lord, and Yours it is to be exalted as Head over all. Both riches and honor come from You, and You reign over all. In Your hands are power and might; in Your hands it is to make great and to give strength to all. Now therefore, our God, we thank You and praise Your glorious name and those attributes which that name denotes (1 Chronicles 29:11–13 AMPC).

I am forever indebted to my awesome, loving husband, Dr. Nwachukwu James Nwabineli. Next to Jesus, you are my most treasured gift. Thank you for carving out time from your hectic work schedule to read and edit early drafts of my manuscript and for giving me advice. You are as important to this book as I am. Your encouragement in rough times is much appreciated and noted. You put up with me with prayer, love, patience, motivation, and encouragement. My heartfelt gratitude, darling. I love you more than I can express in words.

Having an idea and turning it into a book is as hard as it sounds. The experience is both internally challenging and rewarding. I especially want to thank the individuals that helped make this happen. My heart-felt gratitude to my wonderful children, Ngozichukwuka, Chukwu-maobi, Onyedikachukwu, and Charlene for your support, inspiration, and encouragement throughout this project. My special thanks go to my charming daughters Ngozichukwuka and Onyedikachukwu for editing some chapters of the early manuscript. Your input proved invaluable in ensuring this book started and finished well. I appreciate your brutally honest and helpful suggestions and comments. Thank you for being so awesome. Your thoughtfulness is a gift I will always treasure.

I am immensely grateful to Professor Ene Ette for his support, in-terest, and encouragement with editing and proofreading many chap-ters of the original manuscript. I appreciate your prayers, tenacious optimism, keen interest, and helpful advice during the different stages of this project. You were and continue to be an inspiration to me, my wonderful brother in Christ, and one of my most valuable friends for life. God bless you and your family.

Writing a book is hard work, but more gratifying than I could have ever imagined. It would have probably taken much longer to write this book but for well-meaning brethren and friends who encouraged me and insisted I put some of my teachings together into a book for future generations. My deepest appreciation to Professor John and Dr. (Mrs) Funmi Durodola, Honourable Jim and Mrs Ev Cowan, Dr. Ferdinand Nweke, Mr Emmanuel Abuchi Ohia, Prophet Tomi Arayomi, Dr. (Mrs) Funke Arayomi, Pastor Bayo and Mrs Bola Olufemi, Pastor Lois Gott, Pastor Dupe Adefala, Pastor Joycelyn Vassel, Pastors Glyn and Jean Carter, Professor Clara Leyibo Igeleke, Bishop Suzanne Nti, Pastor Joseph and Dr. (Mrs) Kevwe Omoragbon, Mrs Esther Ette, Mrs Pau-line Ogun, Mrs Constance Onyiah, Minister Morin Carew, Mr Patrick Egege, Mr Jonas and Mrs Comfort Abladey, Apostle Enomfon Ntefon, Pastor Toyin Onabowu, Dr. Ikechukwu Joshua and Mrs Chinelo Mad-umere, and Mrs Ihinosen Jane Ajayi. God bless these wonderful peo-ple who make significant efforts to succeed in their own callings and help others to do the same. I am honoured to have you in my life and indebted to you for believing in me. This is genuine love, and it means a lot to me! I thank you for being friends I trust, honour, and respect.

Special thank you to Ms Funmilayo Joy Bafuwa of Heritage Editing Services and Chloe Ford of Credo Communications LLC for their efforts, prayers, encouragement, and personal interest. My sincere gratitude to both of you for your professionalism, amazing editorial expertise, and unwavering support in bringing my stories to life. I am grateful for your sensitivity to the Lord and your devotion to the task.

To all my associates and teams at the Isle of Man Women's Fellowship (IOMWF), Overseas Fellowship of Nigerian Christians (OFNC), National Women's Fellowship, African Missional Community (AMC), Glorious Prayer Eagles (GPE), and the Anointed Praying Mothers (APM): you have each given me the opportunity to lead an elite group of individuals—to be a leader of outstanding leaders is a blessed place to be. I love you all.

To my pastors (Dr. Tim and Mrs Jo Dunnett), all those whose leadership I remotely benefited and still benefit from, my mentors, all the members of the Kingdom Women in Ministry Globally (KWIMG), Our Lady of Lourdes (OLL) alumni group, University of Benin Obstetrics/Gynaecology Residents' Association (UBOGRA), and Women Prayer Altar (WPA), I want to say thank you for being a part of the inspiration and foundation for *Fulfilling the King's Mission*.

I appreciate the individuals in my church family, the OFNC family, that helped make writing this book a reality. Pastor Peter and Mrs Ruth Scott, thank you for your prayers and encouragement. Apostle John and Deaconess Ameobi, Dr. Onyebuchi and Dr. (Mrs) Patricia Eseonu, Mrs Chichi Erharuyi, Mrs Aina Osunkunle, Dr. Kayode Adenekan, Dr. Chikezie and Dr. (Mrs) Ngozi Okike, Mrs Phina Nwoye, Mrs Chioma Nwachukwu, and Mrs Faith George, thank you for making this dream come true in ways you may not even be aware of.

My sincere gratitude to everyone on the Scribe team who helped me so much, especially the ever-patient and most esteemed publishing manager, and the amazing Head of the Scribe team. Special thanks to Tim Beals, publisher of Credo House Publisher, Grand Rapids, Michigan, United States. It was a great pleasure working with you.

Finally, I want to thank everyone who ever said anything positive to me, taught me something, and all those who have been a part of my getting there. God bless all of you.

Foreword

In *Fulfilling the King's Mission*, Dr. Betty Nwabineli delves into who a woman is in the polity, politics, and policing of the kingdom of God. She comes from the perspective of her own experience, living the life of a virtuous woman. Having known her for 30 years, it is not surprising that she approached the book with a passion and zeal to please God with it; and that is part of her DNA.

Dr. Betty Nwabineli makes the case that maximized womanhood is Christlikeness. She brings out the qualities of Christ that every woman needs to emulate in order to be fulfilled. Some of these are bringing pleasure to the heart of the Father, love, compassion, mercy, integrity, truthfulness, wisdom, intelligence, excellence and industry among others. She makes a strong case that you cannot truly serve God without a relationship with Him. She narrates how she tried to serve the Lord without truly knowing Him—a form of godliness born out of religion with no accurate knowledge of our Saviour. All that changed when she encountered Christ in secondary school, and that set her life in a trajectory that only Christ can. You will read her testimony of coming to the Lord and the transformation thereafter. I believe it will challenge you to be sold out to Christ.

Not to be lost in her personal testimony, Dr. Betty Nwabineli brought Sarah and Abigail to life in the pages of the book. By delving into the lives of these two noble and prominent women in the Bible, she highlights qualities and strengths worthy of emulation today. She makes the case that women should operate with Sarah's faith and speak with such wisdom as Abigail who prevailed on David not to kill her husband. You cannot speak with such wisdom without yielding your tongue to the Holy Spirit and hiding the Word of God in your heart (spirit). We cannot associate a loose or careless tongue with a virtuous woman; and the latter is the thesis of this book. A virtuous woman opens her mouth with wisdom, and the bread of idleness (gossip and discontent) she does not eat.

Modelling her life after the virtuous woman of Proverbs 31, Dr. Betty Nwabineli proves that a woman yielded to Christ can be an excellent wife, mother, and entrepreneur. In essence, every daughter of Abraham can become all God designed and created her to be. She has made a passionate appeal for excellence in all that we (men and women) do; and for wives to put their families first, irrespective of any other endeavour they may engage in—the Proverbs 31 model.

As a wife, mother, and grandmother, she called on older women to mentor the younger ones, heeding Paul's admonition. This could not come at a better time, and I encourage young women to study the book and learn from the wisdom and experience of Dr. Nwabineli. Although the book is primarily addressed to women, it also encourages husbands to love their wives in word and deed. I encourage husbands to read it, and not just their wives.

Testimonies of the wonder-working power of God are dispersed throughout the book to remind readers we serve a God of miracles. I encourage readers to take time to study the book and put what they learn to practice in their own lives and to share it with others. As you do, choose the pursuit of kingdom excellence in all areas of your life, and see God amaze you with His blessings. This is the message conveyed in this book; and the book comes with my highest recommendation to you for your study and library.

PROFESSOR ENE I. ETTE
Chief Executive Officer
Anoixis Corporation. Natick, MA

Preface

E very life that leaves an enduring footprint must have a firm foundation and guiding principles worth sharing, so that others may benefit and leave a mark with their own lives as well. Mine is no different. I have written this book by God's grace, partly to share my journey with you dear readers, but also to illustrate the principles that I believe will produce my vision of a kingdom Woman.

I was born into an ordinary family. Unconditional love, uncompromising truth, a sound work ethic, diligence, and the pursuit of excellence were our mantras. I am privileged to have lived most of my life as a Christian. With these two working together, I understand that kingdom life is lived out at the coalface, as they say. Kingdom life is lived out in our callings either as pulpit ministers or in our secular vocations and businesses, a phenomenon now called *marketplace ministry*, which was always the way our Lord Jesus, our perfect example lived and ministered during His time here on earth.

There are different callings for Christians. As a kingdom citizen, it is crucial for you to understand God's unique calling on your life. However, the highest calling in life, the ultimate purpose of being a Christian is to know God and be conformed to the image of His Son, Jesus Christ. To replicate Christ in this world, as temples through whom God lives His life, accomplishes His purposes, and reveals His glory. This is a calling extended to everyone.

Raising our children to fulfil God's plans and purposes for their lives is a serious assignment God has entrusted to every Christian parent. We must raise the next generation to serve their own generation. Therefore, our goal and prayer should be that our godly children raise godly children who raise godly children.

This book encourages Christians to live and serve God understanding who God says He is, who He says we are, and how to serve Him in a way that pleases Him. Knowing that God knows and calls us from the womb, whether male or female, single or married, young or old; we can develop a clear vision of our destination in life.

With God's Word as the foundation, compass, and final arbiter, we should learn from some amazing women in the Bible (Sarah, Abigail, Deborah, Esther, Ruth, Hannah, Mary the mother of Jesus, to name but a few). We should also incorporate the examples and teachings of people like Billy Graham, Oral Roberts, Archbishop Idahosa, Bishop Chris Kwakpovwe, Dr. D.K. Olukoya, Rick Warren, Bishop David Oyedepo, Charles Stanley, Dr. Ferdinand Nweke, Joyce Meyer, John Maxwell, Max Lucado, Ed Silvoso, Kenneth E. Hagin, T.D. Jakes, Kenneth and Gloria Copeland and Joel and Victoria Osteen. Even the Mahatma Gandhis, Martin Luther King Jrs, Mother Teresas, and Nelson Mandelas. We must make an irrevocable decision to allow godly excellence to push us on in our life's journey.

We must always remember what God has done for us as it steadies our faith in His willingness and ability to guide the ship of our life to its haven and destination. I have used my own experiences—the blessings, successes, and victories as well as the challenges and failures to show that this book is practical not theoretical.

Introduction

Work hard and cheerfully at all you do, just as though you were working for the Lord and not merely for your masters, remembering that it is the Lord Christ who is going to pay you, giving you your full portion of all he owns. He is the one you are really working for (Colossians 3:23–24 TLB).

Excellence is never an accident. It is always the result of high intention, sincere effort, and intelligent execution; it represents the wise choice of many alternatives—choice, not chance.   —Aristotle

Foundation for Excellence

The glory of the sun in hot humid afternoons, the rays of sunset and relief of the evening breeze, the rich red soil and tall green trees, joyful ringing laughter and voices that care—these are some of my childhood memories of Nigeria.

Our home was an exciting place. Looking back at the parenting I was privileged to receive, I glorify God unceasingly for my parents. Their graciousness, love, and discipline all contributed immensely to who I am today. I can say with absolute certainty that my parentage was divine. The gracious hand of God was upon me right from when I was conceived.

Before I formed you in the womb, I knew you. Before you were
born, I set you apart for my holy purpose (Jeremiah 1:5 GW).

As a child, I admired my wonderful parents' diligent work ethic.
Over the years, I noticed how devoted they were to every task. They
believed it was their responsibility to be excellent parents and did everything to the best of their ability. Although we were not very wealthy,
we were a close-knit and happy family. Tal Ben-Shahar stated, 'Happiness, not gold or prestige, is the ultimate currency'. We did not have
abundant material possessions growing up, yet by God's grace, we had
everything, hallelujah!

My amiable and audacious mother of blessed memory exhibited
many virtues like the Proverbs 31 woman. Two in particular were
excellence and her altruistic motivation to invest in family, friends,
associates, clients, and others. I learned that investing in people was
not merely about giving money. It was more of helping others identify the resources around them and enabling them to develop their
gifts and talents to maximise these resources. It is wonderful to be
generous with your money. However, if you genuinely care about
someone, you will spend time, love, resources, information, and
correction as well. My mother joyfully and relentlessly poured into
those around her, right from her youth. She came from a polygamous
family and had five siblings, and over ten half-siblings. They were
all recipients of her love and generosity, and she was a huge blessing
to all.

By God's grace, I have done my best to emulate these qualities.
I made altruism and helping people to be their best two of my major
goals in life. I decided to be a woman of excellence and an investor in
people like my wonderful mum. That is one reason I wrote this book.

I find Proverbs 31 extremely inspiring. A beautiful narrative of a
conversation between a mother and son in search of a woman of character whom the son can trust. This is the woman every godly man should
look for, and the goal every Christian woman should strive for. It is not
necessarily a portrait of perfection, but excellence. It shows the value
of inner strength, wisdom, diligence, wise business practices, integrity,
and compassion for the poor. These attributes flow from someone who

trusts completely in God and has earned the trust of God, her husband, children, and dependants.

While *Fulfilling the King's Mission* is a blueprint for kingdom women of excellence, it contains secrets and nuggets that every believer can learn from. The book of Proverbs is a storehouse of practical wisdom, instructions, and recommendations valuable and available to all. Proverbs 31:10-31, portrays a virtuous woman who loves God with all her heart and soul. Thus, she lives with purpose, diligence, and freedom.

There is neither Jew nor Gentile, neither slave nor free, nor is there male and female, for you are all one in Christ Jesus (Galatians 3:28 NIV).

I think this implies that the virtues of this incredible Proverbs 31 woman would sit beautifully on any woman regardless of her race, tribe, age, or background.

Jeff Olson, in his book *The Slight Edge*, summarised a quote usually attributed to Aristotle: 'We are what we repeatedly do. Excellence, then, is not an act, but a habit'. Olson wrote, 'Any time you see what looks like a breakthrough, it is always the result of a long series of little things, done consistently over time'. And Napoleon Hill stated, 'There is one quality which one must possess to win, and that is definiteness of purpose, the knowledge of what one wants, and a burning desire to possess it'.

I believe that life should be lived with purpose, mission, vision, and philosophy. I live by the Word of God, passionately believing in and staking my life on it. I also apply wise sayings, quotes, and ideas from well-known philosophers, writers, etc. Many contain excellent and (in my opinion) godly principles we can live by. Consequently, I have applied Aristotle's and Jeff Olson's theories in many areas of my life. I discovered that truly, the small, seemingly insignificant things we do every day greatly impact our lives in the long run. Like Jeff Olson put it:

Easy to do and easy not to do daily simple disciplines might have no impact on what we do now or tomorrow, but compounded over time, they determine if we are to climb up on the curve of success, or gradually but surely slip down the failure curve. How do you eat an elephant? One bite at a time. How do you go after a big dream? One day at a time—*chopping it up into daily disciplines and visions. Any way you look at it, your future is hidden in your daily routine.*

Hear another brilliant writer:

It is not what we do once in a while that shapes our lives. It is what we do consistently.   —Anthony Robbins

I find Christian Baker's comment on the Aristotle quote remarkably interesting. He wrote:

This is true of everything, success, happiness, fitness, wealth/debt, they are all a result of what we consistently do, our habits, good, bad, positive or negative, our life is created not by the things we do once in a while, but the things we do on consistent basis. Our fitness doesn't come from going for a run once or attending the gym once in a while.

It is crucial that we devote time and effort to plan where we are going in life. I am reminded of the poignant words of Apostle Paul:

I have fought the good fight, I have finished the race, and I have remained faithful (2 Timothy 4:7 NLT).

Although Paul knew death was near, he had no regrets. Why? He had lived with such passion and dedication to the Lord. This Man of God was wise in storing up treasure in heaven instead of here on earth. He gave everything he had to preach the gospel. Paul used every ounce of his God-given gifts to the fullest in order to fulfil this calling.

If we are to experience the abundant life God has for us, we must keep our dreams in front of us. We must see that reason to get out of bed every morning. Realise that you are a person of destiny. You have a purpose on earth. You did not just show up by accident. According to Scripture, God knew you before you were born.

You made all the delicate, inner parts of my body and knit me together in my mother's womb. Thank you for making me so wonderfully complex! Your workmanship is marvelous—how well I know it. You watched me as I was being formed in utter seclusion, as I was woven together in the dark of the womb. You saw me before I was born. Every day of my life was recorded in your book. Every moment was laid out before a single day had passed (Psalm 139:13-16 NLT).

God has an assignment for you. There is something God wants you to accomplish. Someone somewhere needs your love, smile, and encouragement. Your heavenly Father placed you on planet Earth to make a difference, impact your society, and make this world a better place. Inside you are dreams and desires put there by the Creator of the universe. But over time, trials, challenges, and storms of life will try to push those God-inspired dreams down, little by little. It could be a disappointment here, a setback there, a failed relationship or dream that did not work out. If you are not careful, you may wake up one day to realise that you are no longer pressing forward. Are you letting opportunities pass you by? Are you sitting or standing on the side-lines of your own life? This is not the portion of the redeemed of the Lord. Until you recognise that God created and redeemed you for a purpose, other people will try to 'breathe' their identity and agenda into you. That is dangerous because when someone can define you, they can control you. **You must find your purpose and pursue it with passion. Give it your absolute best**.

Be sure you put your feet in the right place, then stand firm.
—Abraham Lincoln

Do not ever make the mistake of telling God that you have nothing to offer. That simply is not true. God does not create any junk.
—Myles Munroe

Remember that God will lead, guide, and prosper everything in His will you embark on. He will pour out His favour and blessings, and you too will fulfil your destiny. Ken Wert asked the questions below in his blog *Stand and be counted. Are you standing on the side-lines of your own life?*:

> If a statue were to be erected in your honour, what would it be sculpted to look like? Would it stand nobly, squared shoulders, strong, facing the elements or would it be nervously slouched as though hiding in the shadows of taller monuments? Would the statue be holding a pen, a ball, a child or lifting a fallen stranger from the ground? Or would it be clutching a TV remote and a bag of chips in its stony hand with the look of boredom dully etched onto its granite face? What would be inscribed on its base? Would it say, "Here sat ..." or "Here slept ..." or "Here shrugged ..."? Or would it instead proclaim, "Here stood ..."?

Let us search our hearts and be brutally honest about what we are utterly committed to in life. What are you willing to devote your time, effort, spirit, and soul to? Emulate those who stand for something great and righteous they believe in. Spend quality time seeking God in prayer until a clear picture of the future is created in your heart. Choose to be drawn forward by that future daily. This will help you push through whatever challenges you encounter in the present, and whatever pulling and clutching you may feel from the past. Since you can neither change the past, nor on your own completely shape the future, it is smarter to be influenced by something you can change rather than something you cannot change. C.S. Lewis is accredited with the following encouraging quote aimed at seniors: 'You are never too old to set another goal, or to dream a new dream'.

I believe that when the revelation of the place of honour and glory that God has assigned to women hits us fully, we will walk in the fullness of our identity and calling. Even men will appreciate the priceless value of the assignment of womanhood. I thank God for the opportunity to share my passion to see people come to the saving knowledge of Jesus Christ. I pray that they find their place in God's kingdom, reclaim, and pursue excellence as their way of life, and succeed in their God-given purpose and kingdom destiny.

It is truly awesome to contemplate that the Almighty is involved and operative in the lives and activities of His people. God's good hand is always clearly associated with provision, power, and protection in our lives and ministry. The phrase *The hand of God* speaks of the reality that God protects and provides for His people. It carries the certainty that He promotes His purposes through His unquestionable authority, power, and unlimited ability. Understanding this ought to instil security and confidence in our hearts. We must also recall the words of our Lord Jesus Christ:

> I give them eternal life, and they will never perish. No one can snatch them away from me (John 10:28 NLT).

May we also never forget that this God Who holds and watches over all of us, His precious children, is the same God:

> Who spreads out the northern skies over emptiness and hangs the earth upon or over nothing. He holds the waters bound in His clouds [which otherwise would spill on earth all at once], and the cloud is not rent under them. He covers the face of His throne and spreads over it His cloud (Job 26:7-9 AMPC).

It is crucial to hold the reminders of God's past help close. This reassures us that His faithfulness continues today, and we can follow Him confidently into the future. Testimonies encourage us to trust God forever and help others know God's hand is all-powerful. The memories of what God has done can become building blocks for trusting God in what He will do now and in the future.

> Let never day nor night unhallowed pass, but still remember what the Lord hath done.   —William Shakespeare

The Psalmist said:

> But then I recall all you have done, O Lord; I remember your wonderful deeds of long ago. They are constantly in my thoughts. I

cannot stop thinking about your mighty works (Psalm 77:11–12 NLT).

In the Scriptures, the Israelites often gathered memorial stones to remind them of specific victories God had given them. Anyone who passed one of these huge markers would recall and retell the wonders of God. In the same way, we need to build memorials in our own lives. Do you take time to relive your victories? Learn to stop and celebrate what God has done in your life and share your testimonies with others. This is one way I build my faith and keep myself encouraged. Remember how God made a way when it looked impossible? When you were so lonely and God brought someone special into your life? Think how God healed you or a loved one. What about that job He gave you? Remember the day your children were born and other miracles. Learn to develop an awareness of God's goodness on the inside, and say, *I know if God did it for me once, He will do it for me again.* We need to be reminded of God's goodness regularly. When you do, your faith will increase, and you will see God's mighty hand working every single day!

This book is a glowing testimonial of God's faithfulness to me and my family. It is also a memorial to encourage me to walk with and serve God all my days. My hope is that it will be a source of encouragement to you. Precious memories of yesterday can strengthen our faith today and tomorrow and also help others.

This book also aims to express the Father-heart of God. It presents both the dynamics and guidelines required to raise kingdom heirs— our future generations. My desire is for heirs of God's kingdom to be appropriately equipped by the power of the Holy Spirit to the standards of the King. I strongly believe that it is our destiny to rule and reign on earth.

> For if because of one man's trespass (lapse, offense) death reigned through that one, much more surely will those who receive [God's] overflowing grace (unmerited favour) and the free gift of righteousness [putting them into right standing with Himself] reign as kings in life through the one Man Jesus Christ (the Messiah, the Anointed One) (Romans 5:17 AMPC).

And hath made us kings and priests unto God and his Father; to him be glory and dominion forever and ever. All glory and power to him forever and ever! Amen (Revelation 1:6. KJV).

As kings and priests, we are to rule. It is not whether we want it: **It is our duty. It is our destiny!**

This is not a book of philosophy or theories. Neither is it a book of spiritual or faith-building techniques designed to *reach God*. God knows each one of us inside and out and is already available to everyone. I pray that by sharing what I have received from God, I can encourage, inspire, and motivate you as you read my experiences, successes, setbacks, struggles, challenges, victories, and some lessons I learned as a Christian (of over fifty years), wife (for over forty-three years), mother, grandmother, and marketplace minister (entrepreneur and career woman).

A lot of the material for this book comes from seminars and sermons shared over several years in various churches and conferences at home and abroad. I pray that God Himself, our inspirational Source, the basis for everything good and worth imitating, imparts His grace for excellence and blesses you richly as you read. I pray you reach out in simple faith like the woman with the issue of blood and take what God has for you in this book. Be encouraged to share the truths, lessons, guidance, and inspiration you glean. In doing so, enhance the lives of God's precious people.

CHAPTER 1

A Woman in Pursuit of God's Kingdom

But seek (aim at and strive after) first of all His kingdom and His righteousness (His way of doing and being right), and then all these things taken together will be given you besides (Matthew 6:33 AMPC).

My testimonies matter, but they are not about me. I understand we live in an age where self is all that matters. Nevertheless, I will do my best to avoid self-adulation. My purpose is to tell the world about the goodness of God. My life displays God's grace, mercy, and favour, not trophies of my accomplishments. My stories tell what God has done and is doing in my life. How He worked to take me from lost to found—a powerful witness of His faithfulness and love. I believe that this may be the very thing that someone else needs to hear to move from lost to found. Not because it is my story, but because it is His.

Salvation testimonies and stories of Christians matter because one person's life can enhance another's. Although unique as individuals, we have the bond of being created by the same God. What Christ has done for one person, may be just what someone else needs to hear, to build faith that God can work in their lives too. I want my testimony to inspire and persuade those who do not yet believe, yet also encourage those who already believe. I pray that God will use my life stories for His glory and give me more opportunities to share them. To God be all the glory, as I trust Him to do so.

How I Came to Know Jesus Personally

Jesus answered him, 'I assure you and most solemnly say to you unless a person is born again [reborn from above—spiritually transformed, renewed, sanctified], he cannot [ever] see and experience the kingdom of God' (John 3:3 AMP).

Growing up with my wonderful parents and eight siblings was joyful. We were a happy family with strong Roman Catholic beliefs. We did many things together. I thank God for my parents, who loved us and would do anything for us. I am the second of nine children, but the first daughter. From childhood until the age of thirteen, I was a nominal Catholic. But when I entered a Roman Catholic girls' secondary school, I became a steadfast, practicing Roman Catholic.

My parents were particularly good people, known by all around. My dad worked in the hospital as a senior nursing officer and my mum was an entrepreneur and Mother in Israel. Their good works were 'sung' in their domain of influence.

Our parents instilled the practice of good works in us. We learnt to be helpful and loving; to 'Do to others as you would have them do to you' (Luke 6:31 NIV). I became as spiritual as possible and did my best to be as devout a Catholic as possible. I even assisted the priests as an altar girl in the college church when altar boys were not available. They knew me in my neighbourhood as *the little good girl*.

In church, we were taught that if you were a good person and did the best that you could, you would go to heaven when you died. In other words, God would only judge me by the good things I did in life. I believed this to the letter.

Many people have dramatic conversion testimonies. Some nearly as dramatic as Saul's Damascus road experience. Others dump horrible habits and lifestyles miraculously with evidence of their new birth glaring in transformed lives. In my case, I was a good person who was hell-bound. In retrospect, I never remember reading or studying the Bible; it was a closed book to me. Growing up, I had my Baltimore Catechism, St. Joseph's Missal (containing the standard Catholic prayers: Mass, confession, the Church calendar of saints' days and feasts, etc.), rosaries, and Mass cards. I cannot recall anyone ever sharing the true Gospel with me. No one explained biblical truths to me until God gave me the grace to hear and understand.

Zealous for God without Knowledge

I must say that from an early age, I had a zeal for God, even as a nominal Catholic. However, I did not know Jesus at all, though I knew a lot about Him. It is extremely easy to be religious without knowing God. I am sure there are still many people who are in that situation today. This was written of the Jews:

> For I can testify about them that they are zealous for God, but their zeal is not based on knowledge. Since they did not know the righteousness of God and sought to establish their own, they did not submit to God's righteousness. Christ is the culmination of the law so that there may be righteousness for everyone who believes. (Romans 10:2–4 NIV).

I needed the righteousness of Christ to save me, and not my righteousness. Inside me, however, God was working. I came to realise that all was not well.

Ignorant of the Gospel

At seventeen, (just before the charismatic renewal swept through the Catholic Church), I had to transfer to Anglican Girls Grammar School (AGGS) Ughelli, in Delta State of Nigeria when the Nigerian Civil War broke out. A Roman Catholic now in an Anglican secondary school!

Many things became different, especially prayers and morning assembly. I thought I had a real belief in God, but never really knew Him. However, still, in search of the truth, I got involved in the Scripture Union (SU) and was happy for a time. But as I got to know a few believers, I realised they had something I lacked. Perhaps it was the words they shared about what they found in the Bible or the way they prayed. I knew I was missing something. More and more, I realised that I did not understand what it meant to be a Christian.

I recall one Scripture Union meeting just before I turned eighteen. The guest evangelist in closing the meeting said the words that would change my life forever. I cannot quote him verbatim, but he said something like, *Are you ready to surrender your life to Jesus Christ, to ask Him to be the Lord and Saviour of your life? There is none righteous, there is none that does good, no, not one. Your good deeds are like filthy rags before God.*

I felt like my heart was breaking into pieces, thinking *my many good works like filthy rags before God?* As he continued, I began to realise that we humans are all helpless to save ourselves—we need an all-powerful Saviour. Every other religion and belief system tells us it depends on us. Whether it is through good deeds, keeping the commandments, carrying out rites and sacraments, working together, thinking hard enough, or making the right decisions, etc. All this is mere deception and lies of the devil. The bottom line is that **you must be born again to go to heaven**.

That was the first time in my life I heard the phrase *born again*. His words penetrated my heart like a divinely directed scalpel. I felt they were spoken to no one else at the meeting but me! How did he know my burden? But bless God, Who helped me to receive the message with meekness, I silently repented and immediately cried out to Jesus to be my Lord and Saviour.

Light Breaking through the Darkness

At that moment, it was as if the light came in and dispelled my darkness. For the first time in my heart, I grasped why Jesus Christ had to die on the cross. I saw that I was not good enough or strong enough to save myself and get into heaven. Jesus, the perfect Son of God, had to die on the cross—carrying my sin and guilt. Only He could fully take the punishment for what I had done wrong and so cleanse me from all my sins. I finally understood that I had been relying on my religious efforts and not upon the completed and all-sufficient sacrifice of Jesus

Christ. No one ever told me that our righteousness is fleshly and not acceptable to God, nor that we need to trust in His righteousness alone.

Until then, I did not even realise that the Bible clearly states we cannot earn salvation; that it is a gift of God, given by His grace through faith (Ephesians 2:8–10). This passage in Titus 3 was another eye opener:

> But when the goodness and loving-kindness of God our Savior to man [as man] appeared, He saved us, not because of any works of righteousness that we had done, but because of His own pity and mercy, by [the] cleansing [bath] of the new birth (regeneration) and renewing of the Holy Spirit, Which He poured out [so] richly upon us through Jesus Christ our Savior. [And He did it in order] that we might be justified by His grace (by His favor, wholly un-deserved), [that we might be acknowledged and counted as con-formed to the divine will in purpose, thought, and action], and that we might become heirs of eternal life according to [our] hope (Titus 3:4–7 AMPC).

I realised in that divinely ordained moment that by receiving God's gift of salvation, I had passed from spiritual death to life. I moved on from having a religion to having a vital relationship with Jesus Christ. Now that I was a believer, I could know Him and fellowship with Him. Jesus invites all humanity to come to Him. If you do not know Him, now is the time to accept His offer.

> Behold, I stand at the door and knock. If anyone hears my voice and opens the door, I will come into him and eat with him, and he with me (Revelation 3:20 ESV).

Water Baptism

I got baptised in a river in Ughelli, out of obedience to my Saviour. In this, I identified with what He had already done for and in me. He had washed me of my sins. With Him, I was buried with my old life of sin and raised again to a new life. That is what baptism symbolises—God's inner work in a child of God. Peter, by the Holy Spirit, gave us insight into the work the Holy Spirit does in us at baptism.

> And baptism, which is a figure [of their deliverance], does now also save you [from inward questionings and fears], not by the removing of outward body filth [bathing], but by [providing you with] the answer of a good and clear conscience (inward cleanness and peace) before God [because you are demonstrating what you believe to be yours] through the resurrection of Jesus Christ (1 Peter 3:21 AMPC).

Shortly after I gave my life to Christ, I received the gift of the Holy Spirit (see Acts 2:38b). In other words, I was filled with the Holy Spirit.

> And they were all filled with the Holy Spirit and began to speak in other tongues as the Spirit gave them utterance (Acts 2:4 ESV).

This took place during a night vigil at the home of our principal. I had this wonderful encounter and spoke in tongues for the first time. Other Scripture Union sisters who attended these prayer meetings had the same experience as well. Something remarkable happened after we were filled with the Holy Spirit. Like the disciples after Pentecost, we became so empowered and fearless that we went to the forest (by the college) with our lanterns to pray after school lights out at 9 pm. We were so full of the Holy Spirit and His power; it was glorious.

People knew the forest was infested with wild animals. We did not remember there was something called fear. We would pray in our understanding and in the Holy Spirit sometimes till midnight. We were not after personal needs, all we wanted and sought God for was more of Him. It was awesome. We were never caught or attacked. It was during one of those nights I had a personal encounter with God and had a touch of His Shekinah glory that further changed my life forever. *This God is too much,* as we say in Nigeria. I can testify that our God is truly ALIVE, and He is the God above all gods.

A Hope and a Prayer—An Invitation

As I conclude this chapter, I would like to ask something of you. I strongly encourage you to give your life to Jesus Christ if you have not already done so. Maybe (like me before I knew the truth), you are relying on your good deeds and efforts to be right with God and enter heaven. Perhaps you may not have a firm belief in God, but you are hedging your bets by relying on your good deeds. I say strongly but lovingly: Do not be deceived!

The Bible states clearly that we have all sinned and come short of the glory of God. And there is nothing we can do to make up that distance between God and ourselves. It is no good saying, *I will do my best and God will take care of the rest.* The Bible tells us:

> For whosoever shall keep the whole law, and yet offend in one point, he is guilty of all (James 2:10 KJV).

All we can do is believe in the One who has done all that was needed for our salvation. Jesus Himself said:

> This is the work (service) that God asks of you: that you believe in the One Whom He has sent [that you cleave to, trust, rely on, and have faith in His Messenger (John 6:29 AMPC).

Keeping First Things First

To experience joy, blessings, and the favour of God, you must put the most important things in life at the top of your list. If you want to experience God's best, put your relationship with Him first. Stay focused on Him and the things that truly matter in life. To reach your potential and become everything God wants you to be, make sure His priorities are yours.

What are you striving for in life? Are you seeking His kingdom? Just as Matthew 6:33 says, when you make God's kingdom your priority, all things will be given to you. If you have been putting other things first, decide right now to change and seek God above all else. As you do, you will experience joy and peace like never before.

Even now, God is calling you with the Gospel—the good news that there is a Saviour. Will you acknowledge your sin and inability to save yourself? Will you turn to the Saviour now? Christ died on the cross, but three days later, He rose triumphantly from the dead. He is ALIVE and sits enthroned in heaven. He hears when we call to Him. The Bible has this wonderful promise:

> That if you confess with your mouth, the Lord Jesus, and believe in your heart that God has raised Him from the dead, you will be saved. For with the heart one believes unto righteousness, and with the mouth confession is made unto salvation. For the Scripture says, 'Whoever believes on Him will not be put to shame.' For there is no distinction between Jew and Greek, for the same Lord over all is rich to all who call upon Him. For 'whoever calls on the name of the Lord shall be saved' (Romans 10:9-13 NKJV).

With all my heart, I say this: Come to the only true Saviour, Jesus Christ. I end with this Bible passage:

> But God clearly shows and proves His own love for us, by the fact that while we were still sinners, Christ died for us
> (Romans 5:8 AMP).

Prayer for Salvation and Baptism in the Holy Spirit.

Please pray in faith if you do not yet know Jesus as your Lord and Saviour and would like to do so.

> Dear Heavenly Father, I come to You today in the Name of Jesus. I believe that out of Your immense love You have created me. In many ways and for many years, I shunned Your love. Thank You, Father God, for sending Your Son Jesus to die for me. I believe and confess that Jesus is the Son of God, and I

believe in my heart that God raised Him from the dead. I accept your gift of life and welcome you into my life. Fill me with the Holy Spirit. Holy Spirit, arise within me as I give God high praise. I fully expect to speak with other tongues as You give me utterance in Jesus's Name. Amen.

....

ESSENTIAL POINTS FROM CHAPTER 1

- For God so loved the world, that he gave his only Son, that whoever believes in him should not perish but have eternal life (John 3:16 ESV).
- Truly, truly, I say to you, whoever hears my word and believes him who sent me has eternal life. He does not come into judgment but has passed from death to life (John 5:24 ESV).

Declaration

By the grace and mercy of God, the Father of my Lord Jesus Christ, I am born again. I now live with great expectation, and I have a priceless inheritance—an inheritance that is kept in heaven for me, pure and undefiled, beyond the reach of change and decay. Not only have I passed from death unto life as 1 John 3:14 says, but this life also comes with a living Spirit that dwells with me and in me. I am convinced that nothing can ever separate me from God's love. Neither death nor life, neither angels nor demons, neither fears for today nor worries about tomorrow—not even the powers of hell can separate me from God's love.

I decree this by faith in Jesus's majestic name!

Further Study and Scripture References

John 14:15; Romans 8:3–9; 1 John 1:9–10, 2:3–6, 3:14, 24, 5:13.

CHAPTER 2

A Kingdom Woman in Pursuit of Excellence

That you may approve the things that are excellent, that you may be sincere and without offence till the day of Christ (Philippians 1:10 NKJV).

Strive for excellence, not perfection, because we do not live in a perfect world.   —Joyce Meyer

Praise for a Kingdom Woman of Excellence

A good woman is hard to find and worth far more than diamonds. Her husband trusts her without reserve and never has reason to regret it. Never spiteful, she treats him generously all her life long. She shops around for the best yarns and cottons and enjoys knitting and sewing. She's like a trading ship that sails to faraway places and brings back exotic surprises.

She's up before dawn, preparing breakfast for her family, and organizing her day. She looks over a field and buys it, then, with money she has put aside, plants a garden. First thing in the morning, she dresses for work, rolls up her sleeves, eager to get started. She senses the worth of her work, is in no hurry to call it quits for the day. **She's skilled in the crafts of home and hearth, diligent in homemaking**. She's quick to assist anyone in need, reaches out to help the poor. She doesn't worry about her family when it snows; their winter clothes are all mended and ready to wear. She makes her own clothing, and dresses in colourful linens and silks.

Her husband is greatly respected when he deliberates with the city fathers. She designs gowns and sells them, brings the sweaters she knits to the dress shops. Her clothes are well-made and elegant, and she always faces tomorrow with a smile. When she speaks, she has something worthwhile to say, and she always says it kindly. She keeps an eye on everyone in her household and keeps them all busy and productive. Her children respect and bless her; her husband joins in with words of praise: 'Many women have done wonderful things, but you've outclassed them all!' Charm can mislead and beauty soon fades. The woman to be admired and praised is the woman who lives in the Fear-of-God. Give her everything she deserves! Festoon her life with praises (Proverbs 31:10–31 MSG).

Proverbs 31 concludes a book of God's practical wisdom, replete with accurate portrayals of human character. It is full of invaluable instructions and recommendations for everyone.

The virtuous wife in Proverbs 31 is referred to as an excellent wife.

An excellent wife is the crown of her husband, but she who causes shame is like rottenness in his bones (Proverbs 12:4 NKJV).

Her character reflects inner beauty, integrity, and strength. Driven by the fear of God, she is full of godly wisdom, humility, purpose, and passion. These are some of the most important virtues in achieving excellence. Without passion, things are done half-heartedly, and may give only partial results. It follows therefore that unless you have a strong desire to achieve your goal, you may never be able to achieve excellence in it.

Responsibility and the incredible work ethic showed by the Proverbs 31 woman remind me of the values instilled by my parents in my early years. This is one reason I find it difficult to tolerate laziness in any form. In my business, I do not allow lazy people around me.

A wife of noble character, who can find? **She is far more precious than rubies** (Proverbs 31:10 BSB) (emphasis mine).

Wisdom is the only attribute described in the book of Proverbs as more valuable than rubies.

Blessed are those who find wisdom, those who gain understanding, for she is more profitable than silver and yields better returns than gold. She is more precious than rubies, and all the things you may desire cannot compare with her. Long life is in her right hand; in her left hand are riches and honour (Proverbs 3:1–6 NIV).

For wisdom is far more valuable than rubies. Nothing you desire can compare with it (Proverbs 8:11 NLT).

Therefore, the pursuit of excellence is essentially the pursuit of godly wisdom. We all need true wisdom. That is why the Word declares:

The reverent fear and worship of the Lord is the beginning of Wisdom and skill [the preceding and the first essential, the prerequisite and the alphabet]; a good understanding, wisdom, and meaning have all those who do [the will of the Lord]. Their praise of Him endures forever (Psalm 111:10 AMPC).

The reverent *and* worshipful fear of the Lord is the beginning (the chief and choice part) of Wisdom, and the knowledge of the Holy One is insight *and* understanding (Proverbs 9:10 AMPC).

Many people link excellence to achievements in academics or sports. Judgment is often skewed on the side of societal recognition or reputational acquisition. **However, the excellence described in Proverbs 31 goes beyond what the woman does. It focuses more on who she is. She cannot be reduced to performance only. Her character is almost certainly a product of living in intimacy with a Holy God.** Dr. Ferdinand Nweke stated:

Excellence is a kingdom hallmark. It is God's very nature, His absolute and undeniable character. Creation itself shows that there is nothing mediocre about God. His attributes and everything in and about Him are excellent beyond imagination. His name, greatness, majesty, wisdom, and promises are all described as excellent (Psalm 8:1). Our God cannot tolerate anything mediocre. God's perfect will is that His saints sense and prize what is excellent.

That you may approve the things that are excellent, that you may be sincere and without offence till the day of Christ (Philippians 1:10 NKJV).

The American Heritage Dictionary defines excellence as 'The state, quality or condition of excelling; superiority'. The word excel is further defined as, 'to do or be better than; to surpass; to show superiority, or to outdo others'. The similarity in these two definitions is the comparison index, where being better than others is the criterion for judging excellence. But this is not what the Bible teaches or what the portrait of the virtuous woman reveals.

In my opinion, **biblical excellence is to pursue and do your best with all your God-given gifts and abilities.** God does not expect Christians to judge excellence by comparing themselves with others or by the world's standard.

We do not dare to classify or compare ourselves with some who commend themselves. When they measure themselves by themselves and compare themselves with themselves, they are not wise (2 Corinthians 10:12 NIV).

Ideally, this should be done without competing, striving to outdo someone else or look better than others. Apostle Paul had many critics in Corinth who thought very highly of themselves. But Paul would not descend to the level of comparing himself or his ministry with others. He brings a careful instruction that Christians should not engage in the worldly habit of boasting publicly or inwardly.

God does not measure your life by comparing you with others. The only measure of your Christian life is the Holy Spirit, who measures you by how Christ-like you are, and how much you obey the Word of God. This was where the Corinthian Christians missed it. They either made themselves the measure of others or made others the measure of their worth.

Genuine excellence grows out of a deepening relationship with God. The more you grow to understand and respond to God's love for you, the more you manifest an excellent spirit. Love should, therefore, be your primary motivation for excellence in tackling common tasks, whether people are watching or not. It is more important to know that God sees your work and will reward you accordingly.

Wikipedia states:

Arete Greek: (ἀρετή), in its basic sense, means 'excellence' of any kind. The term may also mean 'moral virtue'. In its earliest appearance in Greek, this notion of excellence was ultimately bound up with the notion of the fulfilment of purpose or function: the act of living up to one's full potential.

Thayer's Greek Lexicon lists excellence as the Greek word *Arete*, which means 'a virtuous course of thought, feeling and action, virtue or moral goodness'.

Paul says:

Finally, brethren, whatsoever things are true, whatsoever things are honest, whatsoever things are just, whatsoever things are pure, whatsoever things are lovely, whatsoever things are of good report; if there be any virtue (excellence), and if there be any praise, think on these things (Philippians 4:8 KJV).

Excellence grows as we align our thinking and actions with God's. When we are born again, we receive the deposit of the Holy Spirit, and the spiritual genetic ability (DNA) for excellence. How much of this we exhibit depends on how we nurture and grow in it. This is actively done by maintaining an intimate relationship with God in prayer and reading/studying the Bible. Based on these foundations, excellence becomes our lifestyle by consciously and deliberately practising what is best at all times.

In the Scripture above, Paul elaborates practical ways to discipline our minds. When we decide to meditate on God's Word, we put our minds on a diet of excellence. It is the truth of God's Word that helps us to:

> … demolish arguments and every pretension that sets itself up against the knowledge of God and take captive every thought to make it obedient to Christ (2 Corinthians 10:5 NIV).

The desire for excellence should therefore be a pursuit for every disciple of Christ. You have an inheritance in Christ that enables you to exhibit His excellence for the glory of God and not the praise of men. Here are a few Scriptures that underscore why everything you do should be done as onto the Lord with the spirit of excellence:

> Whatever your hand finds to do, do it with your might, for there is no work or device or knowledge or wisdom in the grave where you are going (Ecclesiastes 9:10 NKJV).

> Whether, then, you are eating or drinking, or whatever you are doing, let everything be done to the glory of God (1 Corinthians 10:31 WNT).

God wants you to excel in both inward character and outward behaviour. We must be acutely aware of the limited time we have on earth to serve God and carry out His assignments. This means you must do everything with urgency and excellence. Jesus said:

> I must work the works of Him who sent Me while it is day; the night is coming when no one can work (John 9:4 NKJV).

God has an assignment that only you can fulfil. He has given you an allotted time on earth to get it done, but you must be focused. There are five types of nights that can stop us from serving God: rapture, death, (physical or mental) disability, backsliding, and old age.

The time to exercise your faith is now. The time to serve God with all your heart and all-round excellence is now. Do not delay. Do not deny God the value and benefit of your excellent service. Do not waste or squander your time. It is time to make the best of all you have been given. Listen to the Word of God daily. Do not compare yourself to others. Keep doing what makes you successful. Then you will accomplish your God-given assignment.

Jeff Olson stated:

"Someday my prince will come. . ." Good old Walt Disney. Well, that may have worked out for Snow White. Back here on Earth, it's a recipe for disappointment. In flesh-and-blood life, waiting for "someday" is no strategy for success, it's a cop-out. What's more, it's one that the majority follow their whole lives. Someday, when my ship comes in . . . Someday, when I have the money . . . Someday, when I have the time . . . Someday, when I have the skill . . . Someday, when I have the confidence . . . How many of those statements have you said to yourself? Have I got some sobering news for you: "someday" doesn't exist, never has, and never will. There is no "someday." There is only today. When tomorrow comes, it will be another today; so will the next day. They all will. There is never anything but today.

Reclaiming Excellence as a Christian Virtue

Some people look elsewhere when they see a Christian fish symbol on adverts. This is because the service and quality they received from some Christian businesses proved woefully disappointing. Of course, this does not apply to every Christian business. We must correct this expectation in the Church.

Unfortunately, the subject of excellence is hardly ever talked about in Christian circles, but we should. From a biblical perspective, excellence is unquestionably a virtue every Christian should always pursue. Whatever we do, whether we are doctors, cleaners, accountants, pastors, single, married, parents, or empty nesters, we are called to please God through our efforts.

What Excellence Is and Is Not

Excellence is not a skill; it is an attitude.   —Ralph Marston

I have used several quotes in this book, as I do when I write and teach, jotting down key ideas and insights. This habit has helped me in teaching and writing books. It has also helped me as an entrepreneur where I train people in cake-making/decorating, sugar craft, and catering.

It was extremely helpful, especially when writing my master's and PhD theses in medical microbiology. I wrote the chapters in these and my two published scientific books many times over, improving on them each time and presenting them better than I did before, in a more succinct way without compromising the essence of the thoughts conveyed. This paved the way for excellence in producing excellently written theses and books.

I have continued to apply this habit in business, writing articles on social media, and in leading seminars and ministry. I am still improving so I can do even better in the future. This brings me back to the famous quote often attributed to Aristotle: 'We are what we repeatedly do. Excellence, then, is not an act, but a habit'.

Many of us are probably familiar with this quote. When such a simple statement remains alive for centuries, it is wise to stop, recognise, and understand the power and truth behind the words. This quote should be a guiding principle to building your best life now and learning the lessons of pursuing excellence as a habit.

Authors Caelan Huntress and Frank Herron discovered that the origin of this famous quote usually attributed to Aristotle is Will Durant. Durant tried to explain Aristotle's contribution to philosophy in simple terms. Aristotle's original quote was:

One swallow does not make a summer, neither does one fine day; similarly, one day or brief time of happiness does not make a person entirely happy.

The shorter, more popular version of this quote by Aristotle has become a guide for many in the world today, seeking excellence and success in their lives. This quote implies that it does not matter what people do occasionally. **To achieve excellence, an action must be repeated until it becomes a habit. Success is not one big event that happens in your life. It is a result of daily disciplines that lead to God's perfect will.** Here is another interesting quote:

> Any time you see what looks like a breakthrough, it is always the end result of a long series of little things, done consistently over time. —Jeff Olson

The need for personal development in the Church today cannot be overemphasised. You must continue to listen to God's Word, renew your mind, speak the Word, guard your mouth and heart, and do those things that got you where you are today. These daily habits lead us to God's plan.

Excellence involves action, not just promises or things people hope to accomplish. For instance, rather than projecting confidence, procrastinating, and pretending to be on top of things, people who achieve excellence are competent and proactive.

> If you are going to achieve excellence in big things, you develop the habit in little matters. Excellence is not an exception it is a prevailing attitude. —Colin Powell

Professor M.S. Rao stated:

> You must strive for excellence, not perfection. Perfection is impossible except in scientific laboratory experiments and mathematical applications. Most of the time, emphasising perfection rather than excellence acts as an obstacle to progress.

I could not agree more with Professor M.S. Rao, an expert in this subject, that perfection is a phobia. He stated further:

> When you emphasize perfection too much, you tend to make more mistakes, resulting in failures. However, when you emphasize ex-

cellence, you tend to be comfortable as you find it easier to execute and deliver.

Excellence paves the way for improvement, while perfection paves the way for stagnation, limiting one's creativity and innovation. People often fail to deliver goods when the emphasis is laid on perfection. However, excellence tolerates mistakes and failures, thus allowing people to explore and experiment, and, in turn, paving the way for excellence. Excellence is feasible and possible, while perfection is a fantasy and often difficult to attain. **Excellence is pleasure, while perfection is pressure** (emphasis mine).

We are told more than once in the Bible that Daniel had an excellent spirit.

Then this Daniel distinguished himself above the governors and satraps, because an **excellent spirit** was in him, and the king gave thought to setting him over the whole realm (Daniel 6:3 NKJV) (emphasis mine).

How can we develop this spirit and attitude? I believe it resulted from Daniel's fellowship with God and his sense of identity. In other words, he was filled with the Holy Spirit, which made him so successful. This contributed to his **emotional intelligence** (the ability to recognise his own and other people's emotions). I believe the help of the Holy Spirit contributed to the maturity Daniel displayed in his duties and relating with others and, most important of all, his studious uncompromising stand with God. The key factors in the development of Daniel's character are pointers for every Christian today.

I like Jon Courson's commentary on Daniel 6:3:

Darius realized there was an "excellent spirit" within Daniel. What was this excellent spirit? The Holy Spirit. Daniel interpreted dreams. He prayed with effectiveness. He understood visions. He moved in prophecy. He experienced the miraculous. In other words, he was a man who was filled with the Spirit. That's what made him so successful all the days of his life. In 2 Chronicles 16:9, we read that the eyes of the Lord go to and fro throughout the whole earth, looking for a man in whom He might show Himself strong, whose heart is perfect toward Him. Our Father is still looking for men and women in whom He can show Himself strong—as He did with Daniel.

Daniel faced intrigue and jealousy, common in political circles. But envy and plotting could not stop him from being promoted. His excellence was simply above reproach. When his enemies tried to discredit him, he came under intense scrutiny, but his integrity remained solid. He was rather promoted on the strength of his character and excellence. Even the king became more interested in Daniel and was attracted to his God after the investigation. His enemies could find no wrong in his personal life. This incredible story challenges us to examine our own lives today.

Paul says:

Examine yourselves as to whether you are in the faith. Test yourselves. Do you not know yourselves that Jesus Christ is in you?—Unless indeed you are disqualified (2 Corinthians 13:5 NKJV).

What sins do you struggle with? How can you work on your weaknesses so your life stands up to intense scrutiny by enemies of your progress? It is easier to criticise others than to turn the spotlight on ourselves. Being a disciple means to be ready to submit to the scrutiny of the Word of God at all times. You must allow the Word of God to read you as you read it, so that anything in your heart that grieves the Holy Spirit can be revealed and dealt with. The more you mature in your walk with God, the more you realise you cannot stop asking for the grace that the Holy Spirit supplies to remove hardness from your heart. You cannot stop praying for the cleansing power of the blood of Jesus Christ, and you cannot stop confessing your sins in dutiful submission to the examination of the living Word of God and the Holy Spirit. **A life of excellence will silence your enemies (like in Daniel's case). It will also attract the favour of God that leads to promotion.** (See Psalm 75:6-7.)

Because an excellent spirit, knowledge, and understanding to interpret dreams, clarify riddles, and solve knotty problems were found in this same Daniel, whom the king named Belteshazzar. Now let Daniel be called, and he will show the interpretation (Daniel 5:12 AMPC).

You can make a choice to work with our Teacher, Helper, Paraclete and Comforter, just like Daniel and his friends. As these young men were pressed to compromise their faith, they determined not to defile themselves and it was the right choice. In elevating their relationship with God above the fear of an earthly king, they provided an example for all who seek to experience the unhindered flow of excellence.

Excellence demands personal resolve. You must first decide to be an excellent person before excellence can be deployed in your life. When excellence is a habit, it manifests itself in everything you do. Daniel's decision made him the preferred choice. My prayer is that the Holy Spirit will lead you to make decisions that will attract the favour of God and men in Jesus's majestic name. Amen.

The only person you are destined to become is the person you decide to be.   —Ralph Waldo Emerson

Excellence is a lifestyle driven by conviction and vision, so embrace it. This will affect your relationship with others and breed the confidence you need to explore new horizons, set fresh targets, make new contacts, and build new networks. Let me be clear, excellence differs from oratory loudness or excitement. It is neither charisma nor a sense of achievement. For a Christian, excellence is simply being like Jesus Christ.

God is more interested in who you really are than in how you present yourself or your achievements. **God's will is for us to be the best version of who He created us to be.** Everything else (your job, spouse, or home) is a consequence of who you are. Thus, it is important to submit your heart to the Spirit of God.

Keep your heart with all diligence, for out of it spring the issues of life (Proverbs 4:23 NKJV).

The Parable of the Talents

Many of us are probably familiar with this story:

> Now after a long time the master of those servants came and set-
> tled accounts with them. And he who had received the five talents
> came forward, bringing five talents more, saying, 'Master, you de-
> livered to me five talents; here, I have made five talents more.' His
> master said to him, 'Well done, good and faithful servant. You
> have been faithful over a little; I will set you over much. Enter into
> the joy of your master.' And he also who had the two talents came
> forward, saying, 'Master, you delivered to me two talents; here, I
> have made two talents more.' His master said to him, 'Well done,
> good and faithful servant. You have been faithful over a little; I will
> set you over much. Enter into the joy of your master.'
>
> He also who had received the one talent came forward, say-
> ing, 'Master, I knew you to be a hard man, reaping where you
> did not sow, and gathering where you scattered no seed, so I was
> afraid, and I went and hid your talent in the ground. Here, you
> have what is yours.' But his master answered him, 'You wicked
> and slothful servant! You knew that I reap where I have not sown
> and gather where I scattered no seed? Then you ought to have
> invested my money with the bankers, and at my coming I should
> have received what was my own with interest. So take the talent
> from him and give it to him who has the ten talents. For to every-
> one who has will more be given, and he will have an abundance.
> But from the one who has not, even what he has will be taken
> away. And cast the worthless servant into the outer darkness. In
> that place, there will be weeping and gnashing of teeth' (Mat-
> thew 25:19–30 ESV).

Two servants increased what they were given. They were industrious, reliable, and capable with little and could be trusted with true
riches. Because they proved faithful, the master saw a bright future
ahead for them. With God, faithfulness results in promotion and
greater responsibilities. These wise servants passed a test on a lower

level and were promoted into more substantial assignments. This is the result and benefit of personal excellence.

Judging from the response of the third servant, he was not ignorant of his master's expectations. No pretence, he knew the master expected him to trade with his talent. This master would not accept excuses for laziness or lack of results. It did not matter the odds against his servants, or how impossible it seemed, the master still expected all three to deliver. That was why he was so annoyed with the lazy servant who did nothing. Notice his angry master branded him a 'worthless servant' (ESV) and 'unprofitable servant' (KJV) in Matthew 25:30. *Worthless* and *unproductive* are strong adjectives that graphically express the Lord's sentiment toward people who are talented and possess great potential but never develop them.

The words *wicked* and *slothful* used to describe the third servant in verse 26 are taken from the single Greek word *okneros*. According to Strong's concordance #3636, okneros means 'tardy, i.e., indolent; (figuratively) irksome: grievous, slothful'. In the words of Renner:

> It carries the idea of a person who has a do-nothing, lethargic, lackadaisical, apathetic, indifferent, lukewarm attitude toward life. **This is a strong word, chosen by the Holy Spirit to tell us how strongly Jesus feels about those who are apathetic and lethargic about their spiritual lives and life assignments. Jesus has no taste for apathetic people. People who are lukewarm about their God-given abilities or who are indifferent about their assignments leave a sickening taste in the Lord's mouth. He loves the person, but He strongly dislikes the lazy attitudes that keep them from reaching their maximum potential** (emphasis mine).

The word *unprofitable* is from the Greek word *achreios*, which means useless. Nowadays, we would say *good-for-nothing*. Collin's dictionary. com defines worthless as 'without value or usefulness'. Synonyms are pointless, insignificant, useless, ineffectual. A person described this way is a person whose existence in life is pointless. Renner indicated that such

Is an aimless, purposeless person who contributes nothing to life. This person's value has never been realized because he does nothing but takes up space on the face of the planet. But like everyone else, this person had a choice. He could have become something significant if he had used what was entrusted to him and had done what God asked him to do.

Any time I read the parable of the talents, I am thankful that my parents ingrained in me the importance of diligence, resilience, personal development, and believing in myself. My upbringing propels me to always do my best whether in serving God, people, or any assignment. The Lord expects me to do my utmost to His glory. Anything less equates to mediocrity, which is not what God expects of me. Hear Renny Mclean's conclusion: 'Mediocrity is the enemy of excellence'. Jesus's parable in Matthew 25 shouts this message to all of us!

God Promotes People of Excellence

God promotes people of excellence, not those who settle for mediocrity. I reiterate that the Lord has no taste for apathetic people. God will not promote lazy people even though promotion comes from Him, albeit relative to what He has called each person to do.

> For promotion and power come from nowhere on earth, but only from God. He promotes one and deposes another (Psalm 75:6-7 TLB).

Everyone in their right mind wants to be appreciated and promoted. There is nothing wrong with desiring the benefits of success and prosperity. I believe this is what God wants for you as a born-again believer! **The truth is that, even though promotion comes from God, it is not God who determines whether you are promoted or not. You do.** You choose to be promoted by choosing to develop an excellent spirit like Daniel or the diligent servants in the parable.

In this chapter, I have used examples from the lives of the wise servants, Daniel and his friends, and my own life. The internet is replete with tips and nuggets of wisdom posted by psychologists like Celestine Chua and Professor M.S. Rao that will help you achieve personal excellence in anything, irrespective of your area of interest. I love these *10 Steps To Achieve Excellence in Anything* by Celestine Chua:

- Have the hunger for excellence.
- Benchmark against the best.
- Believe that you can do it.
- Build concrete strategy & plans.
- Learn from the best.
- Do not limit yourself.
- Go all out; Work really hard.
- Focus your efforts.
- Be adaptable.
- Never give up.

Although some principles outlined above are derived from the Word of God, in my opinion, the key characteristics of excellence for a Christian must include **the foundation of identity in Christ, being filled with the Holy Spirit, true humility, full obedience, endurance, and an uncompromising stand on God's Word.** Regardless of how much money you make, where you live, your connections, or skin colour, an excellent spirit will be the true determiner of your promotion. Let this book encourage you to pursue all-round excellence.

Finding Purpose

Dr. Myles Munroe, in his book *Understanding the Purpose and Power of Women*, said, 'When purpose is not known, abuse is inevitable'. Here is one of his most popular quotes: 'The greatest tragedy in life is not death, but a life without a purpose'.

Understanding your purpose becomes a great motivation to strive for excellence. Consider Jesus's response when He was confronted on His way to the cross:

> Pilate, therefore, said to Him, 'Are You a king then?' Jesus answered, 'You say rightly that I am a king. For this cause, I was born, and for this cause, I have come into the world, that I should bear witness to the truth. Everyone who is of the truth hears My voice' (John 18:37 NKJV).

John the beloved is assertive about Christ's unbroken focus:

> He who sins is of the devil, for the devil has sinned from the beginning. For this purpose, the Son of God was manifested, that He might destroy the works of the devil (1 John 3:8 NKJV).

Jesus had a definite purpose in life. John tells us:

> . . . as He is so are we in this world (1 John 4:17 NKJV).

Every believer must have a definite purpose that drives their pursuit of excellence. The divine ultimate purpose of believers is to be conformed to the image of Christ placed in them at conversion (Romans 8:29). However, God also wants His people to discover and fulfil His particular purpose and destiny for their individual lives.

You were born to excel and be known for something special. The question is, do your decisions provide you with opportunities to use your unique gifts and skills? Does the path your heart takes make you happy? Does it create loving relationships? Does using your talent make you glad?

God has given you special abilities for specific assignments in the Body of Christ and the world at large. God designed you to stand out, not to blend in. You are one of a kind, irreplaceable, and original. There is no one like you on the face of the earth. It is crucial to understand this truth to pursue a life of excellence. You are meant to do something that will make you unforgettable. You were born to do something that the world cannot ignore. Each believer owes God a debt of discovering their gifts and talents, discerning their purpose in the Body of Christ, and helping equip other believers so they can ascend to a higher position of strength and maturity. This is precisely what I am aspiring to do with this book.

No matter how small your assignment, if you put your whole life and excellence into it, it will speak and never be forgotten. It is time to be like the apostles, who were known for their 'acts'. **You too must be known for your acts—the vision and assignments you finish with excellence.**

Personal Story: Overcoming a Major Challenge

No one is exempt from difficulties. We all face challenges every day. How we choose to overcome storms and obstacles makes us the people we are. As the saying goes, what does not kill you strengthens you. I believe the success of one person could be the inspiration for someone else. With that in mind, I would like to share this story.

By God's grace, I have overcome many challenges in my life. I got my first professional qualification in the United Kingdom as a biomedical scientist in 1982 and returned to Nigeria the following year. I got a rude shock when the Nigerian Institute of Medical Laboratory Sciences insisted I had to take and pass the Nigerian examination to practice in the country. The British and Nigerian examinations were based on different systems. It was a daunting challenge for me to do this examination all over again.

At that time, I was already successful in my confectionery business. I had three young children and a very hard-working husband to look after. But I rolled up my sleeves and embarked on this gruelling programme. After a few months of serious studies, I was ready.

By God's grace, I excelled in the written and practical examinations. My thesis so astounded the examiners that after defending it in another examination with spoken questions and answers/oral examination (viva), I was recalled to the examination room. When I got there, all the examiners were passing my thesis from one to the other. They unanimously declared that my thesis was amazing and one of the best they had ever seen in the Institute's history and so they wanted to congratulate me. I was instantly offered a job in the School of Medical Laboratory Sciences at the University of Benin Teaching Hospital, which I declined because of my family commitments.

I assure you that difficulties are never meant to stop you. They are designed to strengthen you. When you put your mind to a task and trust in God, nothing He permits will be impossible for you. When you are facing a challenge, the Word of God can lift your spirits and give you a fresh start. God's strength can help you face your fears and achieve the impossible. Praise God!

ESSENTIAL POINTS FROM CHAPTER 2

· Excellence is a kingdom hallmark. It is God's very nature.
· From a biblical perspective, excellence is a virtue every Christian should always pursue.
· Who you are is more important to God than your achievements or how you present yourself.
· God's will for our lives is to be the best version of who He created us to be under His supervision.
· We determine whether we are promoted or not even though promotion comes from God.

Declaration

As a born-again child of God, I am filled with and empowered by the Holy Spirit. I carry the spiritual genetic ability for excellence. I, therefore, decree: I have an excellent spirit. I possess the key characteristics of excellence. I know who I am in Christ. I am full of godly wisdom and the fear of God. I operate in genuine humility, full obedience, endurance, and an uncompromising stand on God's Word. The Holy Spirit is constantly at work in me, both to will and to produce excellence, as per His perfect will. I am a success because I function with the wisdom of Christ and His superabundant grace. My daily pursuit of all-round excellence will lead to my all-round promotion today and beyond!

I decree this by faith in Jesus's majestic name!

Further Study Scripture References

Joshua 1:8; Proverbs 4:23, 10:4, 22:29; Daniel 6:3; Matthew 5:1–6; 2 Corinthians 8:7; Philippians 1:9–10, 4:8; Colossians 3:23; Titus 2:7.

CHAPTER 3

The Kingdom Woman as an Excellent Homemaker

Each of the younger women must be sensible and kind, as well as a good homemaker, who puts her own husband first. Then no one can say insulting things about God's message (Titus 2:5 CEV).

To young women. Be a positive example, showing them what it is to love their husbands and children, and teaching them to control themselves in every way and to be pure. Train them to manage the household, to be kind, and to be submissive to their husbands, all of which honor the word of God (Titus 2:4-5 VOICE).

Difference Between a Homemaker and a Housewife

To fully address this, I searched the Scriptures and the internet. What I discovered was remarkably interesting. The word *wife* is mentioned 407 times in the King James Version of the Bible, and it appears in 370 verses. I found the word *housewife* only in a handful of versions. For example, Titus 2:5 (AMPC) exhorts women to be:

> ... self-controlled, chaste, *homemakers*, good-natured (kind-hearted), adapting and subordinating themselves to their husbands, that the word of God may not be exposed to reproach (blasphemed or discredited)

The same verse in the Good News Translation states:

To be self-controlled and pure, and to be good *housewives* who submit themselves to their husbands so that no one will speak evil of the message that comes from God.

Most translations of Titus 2:5 support the *homemaker* concept as the individual who puts a lot of effort into transforming the house into a home. I have discussed the usage of these two terms to leave behind the confusion and emotional hurt caused to many women over the years.

Homemaker as Opposed to Housewife

Both terms are usually interchangeable, but there might be a difference in emphasis. The word *housewife* focuses on the state of the woman as a wife. The word *homemaker* is gender-neutral while *housewife* is gender-specific. I endorse the concept of a house and a home not being synonymous.

Definitions

Housewife:

Sometimes offensive—a married woman who manages her own household, especially as her principal occupation (Dictionary. com)

A married woman, whose principal occupation is caring for her family, managing household affairs, and doing housework (Oxford Dictionary)

A married woman who is in charge of her household (Webster's Dictionary)

The mistress of a household; a female domestic manager (The British Chambers' Twentieth Century Dictionary [1901])

Homemaker:

A person who manages the household of his or her own family, especially as a principal occupation; A person employed to manage a household and do household chores for others, as for the sick or elderly (Dictionary.com)

A person, especially a woman who manages a home (Oxford Dictionary)

One who manages a household especially as a spouse and parent (Merriam-Webster)

Someone who spends a lot of time looking after their home and family (Collins English Dictionary)

Some women today detest the term *housewife*. They believe it is a mistake not only in its usage but also in its creation. This term is offensive to some, probably because it implies an inferior status or defines a woman's occupation relative to a man. *Homemaker* is more modern and acceptable. It also focuses on creating a home rather than being in a house. It does not add more responsibilities.

Going by dictionary definitions, the responsibilities are broadly similar, but *homemaker* sounds more dignified and encompasses women who manage household chores. While the use of this term does not bother some, others argue that since the woman makes a house a home, she deserves to be addressed by a name that shows her work. Some point out that *housewife* is an old-fashioned word that puts a woman down to being nothing else but the *wife* of somebody, and it takes away their uniqueness. It also cannot acknowledge all the dimensions of work that these women do.

Who Is a Homemaker?

She's up before dawn, preparing breakfast for her family and organizing her day (Proverbs 31:15 MSG).

She is not afraid of snow for her household, For all her household is clothed with scarlet. She makes tapestry for herself; Her clothing is fine linen and purple (Proverbs 31:21-22 NKJV).

I have chosen *homemaker* as a better description for a married woman who manages her household, especially when it is her principal occupation. The thought that a homemaker implies less compared to a career woman is wrong. A prudent, focused homemaker manages her home with efficiency and economy. She takes it seriously and makes her household the centre of her attention. Call it what you like, but homemaking is one of the most important jobs in the world. As a homemaker, you do it all; nurse, event planner, chauffeur, maid, educator, and much more. It can be overwhelming, but you are doing something special that many may never be able to do.

It is interesting to note that Adam, the first man and father of humankind, was the first homemaker. When God created Adam, He referred to His creation as *them* (Genesis 1:27-28). This clearly implies that Eve was in Adam and whatever Adam did, Eve did as well. So, Eve was in Adam when God placed him in the Garden of Eden to tend it (Genesis 2:15-23).

Although not a home as we know it today, the garden was part of the palace of God and the home of our first parents Adam and Eve. It still had to be cared for. When Eve was formed from Adam, God reinforced the role that Eve was already playing while in Adam by calling her a *help meet*, or adapted to Adam.

If the very first human created was given an assignment as a keeper, then there is absolutely nothing wrong with being a homemaker even as a man, although the Bible says a lot more about women being homemakers. Ideally, every Christian woman passionate about pleasing the Father should know how to build, watch over, manage, and keep her home in godly partnership with her husband if she is married. Instead of a dreary chore, homemaking should be a ministry where one can make an impact in society and live a life of worship to God.

By applying biblical values daily, Christian homemakers can take pleasure in their role whether they are single, married, young, old, with or without children, even empty nesters. Both male and female Christians must know the foundational principles and scriptural basis for homemaking. This will help in making biblical choices for wise living.

> Now the Lord God said, it is not good (sufficient, satisfactory) that the man should be alone; I will make him a helper meet (suitable, adapted, complementary) for him (Genesis 2:18 AMPC).

> But there is something else God said is not good.

> Also, it is not good for a person to be without knowledge, And he who hurries his footsteps errs (Proverbs 19:2 NASB).

It is possible for a Christian to choose wrongly and follow the values of an ever-changing world. Such choices will soon starve such a person of time-tested and -honoured instructions, which govern human existence from a scriptural perspective. This will cause a deviation from the path that leads to God's promised blessings. True understanding is a gift only God can give through His Word. This is the reason Solomon asked God for understanding instead of relying on his own.

> For the Lord gives wisdom; from His mouth *come* knowledge and understanding (Proverbs 2:6 NKJV).

The Bible was written that we might have understanding and be able to interpret life the way God does. In the absence of knowledge, understanding, and conviction of biblical doctrine, a Christian can easily be led astray. Knowledge, understanding, and application of Scripture will make any Christian woman an excellent homemaker. We risk being misinformed if we are not correctly informed and instructed by the Word of God. David said:

Through Your precepts I get understanding; therefore I hate every false way (Psalm 119:104 NKJV).

Apostle Paul, who wrote much of the New Testament, told Timothy:

Consider what I say, and may the Lord give you understanding in all things (2 Timothy 2:7 NKJV).

Just as Eve was a suitable helper for Adam, knowledge is a suitable helper for people. Knowledge of what God says about homemaking enables us to appreciate its value and virtue. For any Christian woman, submitting to the discipline of God's Word and making it the ultimate authority in her life, is the only way to appreciate what is important, eternal, and brings glory to God. Thus, she will come to understand that being the keeper of her home makes her special.

Creed of the Kingdom Homemaker

- She gains knowledge.

  Through skillful and godly wisdom is a house (a life, a home, a family) built, and by understanding it is established [on a sound and good foundation], and by knowledge shall its chambers [of every area] be filled with all precious and pleasant riches (Proverbs 24:3-4 AMPC).

- She builds her own home.

  Every wise woman builds her home but the foolish one tears it down with her own hands (Proverb 14:1 AMPC).

- She watches over her home.

  She watches over the affairs of her household and does not eat the bread of idleness (Proverbs 31:27 NIV).

46

- She manages her home.

> Besides, they get into the habit of being idle and going about from house to house. And not only do they become idlers but also busybodies who talk nonsense, saying things they ought not to. So, I counsel younger widows to marry, to have children, to manage their homes, and to give the enemy no opportunity for slander (1 Timothy 5:13–14 NIV).

- She keeps her home.

> Older women similarly are to be reverent in their behaviour, not malicious gossips nor addicted to much wine, teaching what is right and good, so that they may encourage the young women to tenderly love their husbands and their children, to be sensible, pure, makers of a home [where God is honoured], good-natured, being subject to their own husbands, so that the word of God will not be dishonoured (Titus 2:3–5 AMP).

I have faith in this 5-point creed. And I believe your work as a Christian wife is largely at home and building a successful home is pleasing to God. Think about it; this is the role given to you directly by God Almighty. It also applies to all unmarried daughters and granddaughters who need to learn how to be keepers at home. I am aware of cultural diversities and contradictory traditional and spiritual narratives on the role of women, but my focus and major resource are the Scriptures, as I am addressing Christians. However, these principles would benefit anyone who applies them.

The concept of family is under siege. What we have known as a model for nurture and impartation of godly knowledge to children now faces many challenges as the world becomes more secularized, values change, and the goal posts shift regularly. Unfortunately, definitions of family are coming under increasing pressure. These issues are often talking points in conferences and workshops and in moral and ethical debates.

I believe God instituted marriage and established the family. He should be the ultimate guide of its focus and direction. As kingdom people, we should adopt His principles for a successful marriage, family, and life.

As a married kingdom woman, you cannot shirk the responsibility God has placed on you for managing your home. Like the Proverbs 31 woman, you set the pace for excellence and a godly work ethic alongside your husband. Kingdom husbands must never think they are just helping their wives in this. They must understand that husbands and wives work as a team for the benefit of the family, because this is exactly how God envisions it. That said, wives should accept that God specifically calls His daughters to homemaking because it interests Him.

Homemaking is God's idea and an integral part of your role, whether single or married. It goes beyond cooking, cleaning, and decorating. It is creating an atmosphere where all can enjoy the goodness and beauty of God, where friends and family experience well-being and a sense of belonging. It also embraces showing hospitality to all, as the Bible admonishes. So godly homemaking is about building homes, where God's kingdom and grace can flourish.

Biblical Homemaking

In Titus 2, Paul instructs older women to teach young women to be keepers at home. What does this mean? The Greek word translated *keepers at home* (KJV) or *homemakers* (NKJV) is *oikouros*. This is a compound word from *oikos* (house, family, household) and *ouros* (keeper, watcher, warden, or guard). Thus, the meaning of the Greek word *oikouros* is a keeper at home, one who looks after domestic affairs with prudence, focus, and care. Let those words sink in for a moment—**prudence, focus, and care**! More significantly for us today is the 'guard' element that this word describes. The Lord is saying He wants us to be watchful over the affairs of our households and to earnestly be on guard over our families.

Apostle Paul is also clear about the need for young people to learn how to live right. They need to be taught by older people, especially those whose lives have been guided by God's Word. He points out that right thinking leads to right living. Although Paul's instruction in Titus 2:3–5 is addressed to older Christian women, in my opinion, it also suits older Christian men. Older kingdom people ought to be living up to the maturity and wisdom of their years. They should be responsible for equipping, encouraging, and empowering the younger ones by teaching and example.

Paul emphasises wives' duties and responsibilities in domestic affairs. He concludes poor homemaking has implications beyond creating a dysfunctional family. It can also lead to the Word of God being blasphemed by the ungodly. However, there is nowhere in the Bible where men are forbidden from working as a team with their wives in domestic matters.

Ideally, a family should function as a team. One difficulty society faces is that the talent for homemaking is often not explored or expressed, and sometimes it is not taught even among Christian mothers and their children. This should be of great concern to all Christian mothers.

From research and interactions with both young and older women, many women (single and married) have shied far away from God's will as far as homemaking is concerned. God's ideals and plans for Christian homemaking have suffered a serious blow because of a shift from internal beauty to external adornments. God does not place as much emphasis on the external as on the hidden man of the heart, which is incorruptible and of great price in His sight. Peter teaches on the law of the hidden person of the heart, saying:

> Wives, likewise, be submissive to your own husbands, that even if some do not obey the word, they, without a word, may be won by the conduct of their wives, when they observe your chaste conduct accompanied by fear. Do not let your adornment be merely outward—arranging the hair, wearing gold, or putting on fine apparel—rather let it be the hidden person of the heart, with the incorruptible beauty of a gentle and quiet spirit, which is very precious in the sight of God (1 Peter 3:1–4 NKJV).

Nowadays, we have tools and gadgets that were not available in years gone by. These make our lives easier and more efficient. Often, some mothers do everything themselves at home without allowing their daughters to work alongside them and learn. It is time to embrace godly homemaking principles and start teaching our daughters and granddaughters how to care, manage, and be keepers of their homes for the glory of God. Where possible, sons and grandsons should not be left out of it, too.

I would like to share from my years of being a married woman, mother, and homemaker. This is to show how homemaking plays a key role in what we do as Christians, whether single, married, young, or old. I hope you see that no matter how insignificant daily tasks may seem to you, homemaking for both Christian women and men is significant before God. My aim is also to motivate you in the areas where you struggle and give you valuable ideas.

Growing up, my mum involved her children in her personal life, homemaking, and business. As the eldest daughter there were times I thought I was being punished because I felt she gave me responsibilities far beyond my age. My parents believed in me and encouraged me. Having my parents instil their own faith and confidence in me shaped the person I have become today. I owe God a debt of gratitude for their investment in my life. They taught me resilience and fortitude, and how to play to win in the journey of life. My mum's sound counsel that I should keep myself undefiled before marriage, amongst other things, helped me immensely. She also taught me the virtue of cleanliness. The training and influence of my parents have played a pivotal role in my life and contributed significantly to who I am today.

I realised early in my marriage, that my children's upbringing was important to me, and that they are my future rewards. I felt I owed them a duty to do for them what my mother did for me. It was not enough for me and my husband to just meet our children's basic needs (food, shelter, clothing, love, care, protection, education, etc.). We committed to going the extra mile to invest in their lives. With God's help, we have raised our children to know and love God, discover their talents, and unlock their potentials. This is the best legacy any parent can bequeath to their children. We spent time with them as they grew up and taught them to seek first the kingdom of God and identify and pursue their passions. They are now godly, responsible, well-educated adults who continue to serve God and excel in their chosen careers—by God's grace.

Becoming an Excellent Homemaker

A career is a vocation, job, or means of livelihood. Therefore, Christian women (single and married) should feel confident in seeing homemaking as a wonderful career, great privilege, and calling.

Homemaking is an art to be mastered, understanding the difference between a house and a home. A home is not defined by its contents. Rather, excellent homemaking involves cultivating the habit of holiness, separating yourself to a life of unconditional love and building healthy relationships with your family. A house can have the most beautiful furniture, equipped with the latest appliances, and yet remain a shell. In contrast, the poorest home with few possessions can be a place of overwhelming love and compassion.

The family home is meant to be a haven, anchorage, and shelter where people experience unconditional love and acceptance. A home is for intimacy and true fellowship. This is the reason making excellent homes should be a wonderful aspiration for everyone.

It is important to be balanced in our approach to homemaking. For example, a woman who keeps an immaculate home may insist guests remove their shoes before entering her home. Shoe removal is a subject so hotly debated that it recently ignited a fiery discussion on a parenting website. It is an issue that everyone has an opinion about. Hosts who apply this rule may be concerned about dirt and potential pathogens. What about infections that the guests might pick up from walking barefoot on carpets and wooden floors that the homeowner and other barefooted guests have been trampling on? Not everyone wears socks or tights.

On a personal note, I would never ask guests to remove their shoes because that seems rude. This amounts to telling my guests that my floors are more important than their comfort. Our carpets are not of greater worth than guests. I am not talking about shoe removal for religious or cultural reasons; I respect that. Some homeowners have no reason to make such a request except that they do not want visitors to mess up their carpets. I have beautiful rugs in my hallway for people to wipe their shoes on before stepping into my living room. By God's grace, my home is well known by friends and family as being immaculate, and most people usually take off their shoes of their own volition. When they insist, even when I ask them not to, I do not fuss about it. I sometimes provide slippers instead.

My home is named *Bethel* meaning *House of El* or *House of God*. We consider our home a place people enjoy visiting and feel comfortable, not a museum. My husband and I do not fuss over guests not taking off their shoes especially since our home is a place of grace, love, and fellowship. Sensible guests do not need to be reminded to take off their muddy or wet boots and jackets on a snowy or wet day before entering any home. Otherwise, the Holy Spirit will help you tell them politely to do what is right.

On the other hand, another woman's home looks as if a cyclone had just struck in total confusion and disorder. These are extremes and we do not honour God in either an unkempt or restrictive home. 1 Corinthians 14:33 reflects a God of peace and order, so there must be balance. The right balance is to learn and apply God's principles for building a happy home. The application begins with realising your worth as a believer. Christ in you makes you an embodiment of grace, a container of divine help, and a carrier of God's kindness to your family and friends.

Once you accept the responsibility for creating an atmosphere of love in your home, cultivate calmness and a peaceful demeanour. Do not be hysterical in reacting to problems. A woman of God and a vessel of honour cannot at the same time be a panicking, overwrought person, because hysteria and fear will paralyse faith.

When God saw man required help, happiness, and deep satisfaction, He created the woman. I believe it is not beyond imagination that God could have helped man directly if He wanted to. He chose, in His infinite counsel and wisdom, to channel all the help, favour, and grace through the life of the woman, and then gave the woman to the man.

Should Married Christian Women Pursue Careers?

This question is controversial and often provokes a lot of intense discussions among Christian women, whether single or married. Christian families struggle with this question around the globe. To answer it, every believer should hold the Bible as the ultimate arbiter upon all matters. The two most highly acclaimed Scripture references mentioning women working outside the home are 1 Timothy 5:11–15 and Titus 2:3–5. Even among Christians who believe these verses of Scripture are God's instruction to married Christian women, there is still some debate.

In verse 14 of 1 Timothy 5, Paul instructs young widows, who are still of childbearing age, to remarry, bear children, keep house, and refrain from idleness. He writes:

> Therefore, I want younger widows to get married, bear children, **keep house**, and give the enemy no occasion for reproach (1 Timothy 5:14 ESV).

> Therefore, I want younger *widows* to get married, have children, **manage their households,** *and* give the enemy no opportunity for reproach (1 Timothy 5:14 NASB) (emphasis mine).

To answer the question above, pastor Stephen Armstrong of Verse by Verse Ministries International (VBVMI) wrote a beautiful article titled *What Does the Bible Say About Mothers Working Outside the Home?* Let us look at an excerpt from his article. Referring to 1 Timothy 5:14, he wrote:

> Based on the context of this passage, we see Paul is concerned about idleness among younger women, who lack a purpose or opportunity to serve others. In Paul's day, women served society primarily by caring for a husband and family, and women had few options for working outside the home.
>
> Therefore, a young widow who remained single might find herself with little or nothing to occupy her days, and she would almost certainly become a financial burden on others in the church

... To avoid this situation, Paul commands young widows to "keep house."

...

Fast forwarding to the modern world of today, single (and married) women have many other options to avoiding idleness and dependence on others. Therefore, we know marriage is no longer the only path to godliness and usefulness.

In light of these cultural changes, we must consider whether Paul's command for single women to marry and work in the home are still relevant today? Can a woman seek employment outside the home without violating the instructions of 1 Tim 5?

In Titus 2:3–5, Apostle Paul again teaches that young married Christian women should be workers at home.

Older women likewise *are to be* reverent in their behavior, not malicious gossips nor enslaved to much wine, teaching what is good, so that they may encourage the young women to love their husbands, to love their children, *to be* sensible, **pure, workers at home**, kind, being subject to their own husbands, so that the word of God will not be dishonored (Titus 2:3–5 NASB) (emphasis mine).

Paul's wording in this passage is similar to the one in 1 Timothy 5:11–15. He suggests a married Christian woman should work to create order in her home. Paul is stressing the importance of a godly woman's responsibility to attend to the duty of running her household.

I refer to pastor Stephen Armstrong of VBVMI again. He stated:

Paul is asking women to embrace the role of overseer in a home, which is the role God has assigned women to the benefit of themselves, the family and society as a whole. Overseeing the home environment is an honorable and essential mission worthy of a woman's pursuit.

Paul's instructions in Titus 2 are much harder to dismiss as culturally obsolete than his instructions in 1 Tim 5. For example, Paul says that young women should be encouraged by older, more mature women to love their husbands and to love their children. Certainly, these commands are still in effect today and not dependent on culture.

Later in the passage Paul says women are to be workers at home, and that they are to be subject to their husband's authority. Once again, we know that the authority of a husband over a wife remains a biblical imperative today, so can we reasonably conclude that only the command for women to oversee the home has expired yet the other commands have not?

This man of God is suggesting that it is rational to conclude that Paul intended the instructions in the two Scriptures above to be as timeless as the rest. Both Scriptures teach that it is God's desire for every godly woman to fulfil her homemaking duty.

Stephen Armstrong further stated:

As long as there are families and households, women are appointed by God to oversee the affairs of the home . . . God created woman with this mission in mind, and so He blessed them with the temperament, sensibilities and instincts best suited to meet the challenges of this role.

So if a woman is God's appointed caretaker for the home, the question remains can a woman meet this responsibility while also accepting employment outside the home?

An answer is found in Proverbs 31:10-31. . . . In summary, Solomon says an "excellent" wife works both inside and outside her home to ensure the sanctity and orderliness of the home environment. This passage strongly supports the conclusion that a woman may fulfil her duties in caring for the home while also seeking outside employment. In fact, employment outside the home can directly support the needs of the household when balanced with her duties inside the home, and Scripture praises such a woman!

The reality is that women have worked outside the home since time immemorial. The Bible mentions women who worked in:

- Commercial trade (Proverbs 31:16a, 24; Acts 16:14)
- Agriculture (Joshua 15:17–19; Ruth 2:8; Proverbs 31:16b)

It also mentions women who work as:
- Millers (Exodus 11:5)
- Shepherds (Genesis 29:9; Exodus 2:16)
- Artisans, especially in textiles (Exodus 35:25–26; Acts 18:1–3)
- Perfumers and cooks (1 Samuel 8:13)
- Midwives (Exodus 1:15)
- Nurses (Genesis 35:8; Exodus 2:7; 2 Samuel 4:4; 1 Kings 1:4)
- Domestic servants (Acts 12:13)
- Professional mourners (Jeremiah 9:17)

Women could also be patrons (Acts 16:40; Romans 16:1-2), leaders (Judges 4–5; 2 Samuel 20:16), and ruling queens (1 Kings 10:1; Acts 8:27). The Bible records one woman who even built towns (1 Chronicles 7:24)!

Many women and men worked from home, yet the Bible nowhere disapproves of women who worked in the public sphere. No matter what jobs kingdom wives do outside the home, the family must be priority number one. All kingdom women—single or married—even if they have a job outside the home, must always remember that they are the makers and keepers of their homes. God has beautifully and wonderfully equipped you for this task. You, as the woman of the home, set the tone.

It is sometimes necessary for Christian wives to work. Some wives can work part-time or even full-time and not neglect their husbands, children, or homes. One of the major issues usually at the core of this discussion is money. This discussion arises where the time required to meet the financial needs of the family puts pressure on the time needed to meet the demands of parental care for the children. There is no universal answer for this.

Women must work for many reasons. Sometimes, the husband is unable or unwilling, or they are single parents. Unfortunately, some couples value a wealthy lifestyle more than the needs of their children. The bottom line is that parents need to realise that God looks at their children as blessings from Him, and they ought to be more committed to the responsibility of raising their children than being financially well-off.

If being a wife, mother, and homemaker is your heart's desire, then know God does not oppose you. It is, in fact, the Lord's calling on your life. There are, however, other viewpoints because the Bible does not specify that only men should work or provide for the family. The Proverbs 31 woman is the best example of a woman being as much a provider for the family as the man. Examples in today's world could include a husband taking study leave to further his skills and improve his career. At such times, the wife may need to work to support her husband.

I recall that several years ago; I worked full-time to support my family. My husband's scholarship ended prematurely, and I was not willing to allow his training to be truncated. I had to work to provide for our family. Women will need to provide if their husbands cannot do so because of ill health, death, abandonment, or one pay cheque being insufficient.

When a wife is pregnant or following the delivery of a baby, the husband might become responsible for domestic chores, besides meeting the family's expenditures. Sometimes, husbands will need to raise children single-handedly in the instance that their wife cannot (because of death, abandonment, etc.). God understands all these situations.

I love the way Barbara Rainey brilliantly summarises this topic in the book titled *Starting Your Marriage Right: What You Need to Know and Do in the Early Years to Make It Last a Lifetime* that she co-authored with her husband Dennis. She wrote:

> I am not opposed to women working outside the home. But I want to discuss the issue of mothers—especially those with young children—devoting time and energy to another full-time occupation. A majority of mothers now work outside the home either part-time or full-time. Reasons include survival needs, lifestyle needs, and personal fulfilment needs. Some women work because they fear a possible divorce would leave them unable to provide for themselves.
>
> Let's look at what is taking place in our culture.

Working mothers are not a new phenomenon. What is new is the shift in career focus: from full-time mother with a job on the side to a full-time career while attempting to mother in whatever time is leftover. I don't believe Scripture supports this notion. A familiar passage in the New Testament summarizes what young wives and mothers are to do: "To love their husbands, to love their children, to be sensible, pure, workers at home, kind, being subject to their own husbands, that the word of God may not be dishonoured." (Titus 2:4–5). Notice the priority of commitments given women in this passage: husband first and children second. Based on this instruction, I think every woman needs to ask herself, 'Is a job the best use of my time? Will, I have more influence on the future through my employment or my children?'

I could not agree more with Lauren Eberspacher that women are intelligent, gifted, and can work anywhere. But the question any Christian wife/mother must ask when faced with the decision to work outside the home part- or full-time is, **is it the best thing for the family in this season? Does my job encourage the growth of my family and does it glorify the Lord?** Take the next important step of praying sincerely about it. Sit down with your husband (if married), close and trustworthy kingdom friends, pastors, and mentors and seek God to know His perfect will for your family. Consider this promise:

> Keep on asking and it will be given you; keep on seeking and you will find; keep on knocking [reverently] and [the door] will be opened to you. For everyone who keeps on asking receives; and he who keeps on seeking finds; and to him who keeps on knocking, [the door] will be opened (Matthew 7:7–8 AMPC).

The truth is, when we are genuinely seeking God's will in any situation, He will remain true to His promise in the Scripture above and lead us in the right direction concerning any issue. The benefits of walking in the Lord and constantly yielding to the Holy Spirit, are immeasurable. Praise God! Here is another powerful promise:

Whether you turn to the right or to the left, your ears will hear a voice behind you, saying, 'This is the way; walk in it' (Isaiah 30:21 NIV).

Here is an inspirational excerpt from Lauren Eberspacher's blog titled *Is It a Sin to Be a Christian Woman and Work Outside the Home?*:

In 1 Corinthians 10:23, Paul writes, *"Someone may say, 'I'm allowed to do anything,' but not everything is helpful. I'm allowed to do anything, but not everything encourages growth."* I believe that this is true in the case of women working outside of the home. In this day and age, Christian women *can* and *are able* to work outside of the home; we are intelligent, gifted, and often times educated women who love the Lord. But the question we each have to ask ourselves is this: is it the best thing for *our* family in this season? Does my job encourage the growth of my family and does it glorify the Lord?

. . . So to the single mother working her fingers off to provide for her family, who longs to be home with her children, but the choice is not hers to make—keep working.

To the wife who picks up an extra shift to help make up for the increased cost of monthly health insurance—keep working.

To the woman who is educated and gifted and truly loves her job—keep working.

To the wife who is working hard to save money before she and her husband start trying to grow their family—keep working.

To the wife who goes back to work while her husband battles sickness and injury at home—keep working.

And to the stay at home wives and moms who wipe bottoms, cook meals, scrub floors, and sit in the school pick up lines—keep working.

And remember ladies, you can, **"be sensible, pure, workers at home, kind, being subject to your husbands, that the word of God may not be dishonoured,"** (Titus 2:5) and at the same time, **"work with eager hands . . . provide food for your family . . . and work vigorously . . . while being profitable"** (Proverbs

31:13-18). What matters is that you are putting God first and seeking His will with your entire heart—there is nothing more black and white than that.

As kingdom people, we must never place our jobs or the love of money before our relationships with God or the well-being of our family.

I also find Marg Mowczko's conclusion noteworthy. In her article titled *Busy at Home: How Does Titus 2:4–5 Apply Today?* she wrote:

> The Bible never tries to make the case that women should not work or have influential roles outside the home. The Old and New Testaments show us that many godly women were not confined to the domestic domain. New Testament women such as Lydia, Priscilla, and Phoebe worked, travelled, and had influential leadership roles in ministry. Paul did not identify these women primarily by their family relationships or their domestic situations. Instead, they are described and identified by their work, their travels, and their ministries.

As previously mentioned, the Bible has never condemned Christian women working outside the home. That said, the Bible does not release a woman from her duties to the home either. Her family and home should always be her priority. That is why, in my opinion, it is unfair for a man to insist that his wife works either part- or full-time or not at all. That should be a decision agreed to by the couple based on scriptural principles (not literal translation) and the particular circumstances of the family.

I agree with Marg Mowczko's opinion in her blog that Paul's instructions in Titus 2:4–5 and in 1 Timothy 5:14 were specifically related to young women of childbearing age and is similar to instructions, also concerning young wives, that were written by pagan authors of the time. Paul's instructions directly reflect the cultural values of his day. And since his words relate to women in a culture different from ours, some of it may not directly apply to all women. What matters is that the principle behind his instructions explicitly summarises what Christian wives and mothers ought to do. These wonderful biblical truths are relevant even in this day and age.

Older Christian women are supposed to teach the younger women to live lives that glorify God. Regrettably, even in the Christian community, aspects of feminism misinterpreted and misunderstood oppose and stifle these truths. The most important thing is that every teacher must seek the help of the Holy Spirit for proper understanding before attempting to teach, to ensure that a clear message is relayed.

Some Christian mothers are forced to work outside the home today because of selfish and stingy husbands. Some husbands deliberately manipulate their wives into financial dependence, a form of financial and emotional abuse. I have counselled wives who are not allowed to work to supplement the household income, even though their husbands' income is inadequate to meet existing needs.

Although distressing instances exist where women work to provide for their families (because of unhealthy situations), many women today deliberately plan a career of full-time work even before they get married. After they get married and have children, they drop babies off in day-care as mum resumes her career. They do this for the next child until she completes her family. The consequence is that babies, sometimes as young as six months old, are dropped off as early as seven in the morning and may not be picked up until seven in the evening. That means someone else is caring for the children twelve hours a day. This delegates mothering and nurturing duties to nurseries and babysitters, and such women miss most major milestones, such as the first smile, which is one of the most rewarding moments of parenthood. Other missed opportunities include seeing babies sitting up unsupported, taking their first step, or even hearing the child's first meaningful word.

Mothers should be the ones to see most of their infants' *firsts* and then deliver the cheerful messages to dads. Unfortunately, many sacrifice all these beautiful moments for a career and pay cheque, even when other options are workable. Sadly, the mother gets to hear second-hand from someone else the special treasures God meant for her.

A kingdom marriage should (from the perspective of the Holy Scriptures) be a valuable partnership and a caring covenant between two adults of the opposite sex. This is built on a foundation of trust, love, and peace, under God's guidance and endorsement. The couple work as a team. They are not meant to be in a competition. Members of a team do not help each other to make the team successful. Rather, they work together as a team to succeed. In a marriage, husband and wife work together for the success of the relationship. The Bible says they are one flesh.

> But if anyone does not provide for his relatives, and especially for members of his household, he has denied the faith and is worse than an unbeliever (1 Timothy 5:8 ESV).

Whilst the woman's priority is to manage and organise the home, the husband's priority is to provide the finance. In families with small children, the most convenient way to do this is for the wife to stay at home and the husband to work. This division of labour makes sense as women often have a better disposition to care for young children, while men culturally find it easier to go out and make money.

However, every family is unique. For example, a disabled or underemployed husband may let his wife be the principal wage-earner. In such a case, he is still responsible for making sure he cares for his family. He just happens not to be the one bringing home the money. Similarly, if the wife works, she still needs to make sure the house runs smoothly. She may delegate tasks to family members according to schedule and inclination, but it remains her responsibility.

Christian Mothers Should Use Their Talents

Another background issue at the core of the discussion of whether a Christian mother should work outside the home is a woman's worth and place in the world. Work provides opportunities for satisfaction, praise, and the qualitative joy of reaching set goals. It takes a powerful personality to find the same satisfaction in being a stay-at-home mother. If this is God's will for any woman, it will take His grace and great submission, self-sacrifice, and humility for the woman to accept underutilization of her education and workplace potential. Lydia (Acts

16:14) and Priscilla (Acts 18:2–3), were both businesswomen and godly examples of women in the church. So, it does not mean women are to just sit at home cooking and cleaning all their lives.

The English Standard Version of Proverbs 31:10 describes the woman in this passage as an excellent wife. Verses 10–31 of this chapter reads:

An excellent wife who can find? She is far more precious than jewels.

The heart of her husband trusts in her, and he will have no lack of gain

She does him good, and not harm, all the days of her life.

She seeks wool and flax, and works with willing hands.

She is like the ships of the merchant; she brings her food from afar.

She rises while it is yet night and provides food for her household and portions for her maidens.

She considers a field and buys it; with the fruit of her hands she plants a vineyard.

She dresses herself with strength and makes her arms strong.

She perceives that her merchandise is profitable.

Her lamp does not go out at night.

She puts her hands to the distaff, and her hands hold the spindle.

She opens her hand to the poor and reaches out her hands to the needy.

She is not afraid of snow for her household, for all her household are clothed in scarlet.

She makes bed coverings for herself; her clothing is fine linen and purple.

Her husband is known in the gates when he sits among the elders of the land.

She makes linen garments and sells them; she delivers sashes to the merchant.

Strength and dignity are her clothing, and she laughs at the time to come.

She opens her mouth with wisdom, and the teaching of kindness is on her tongue.

She looks well to the ways of her household and does not eat the bread of idleness.

Her children rise up and call her blessed; her husband also, and he praises her: "Many women have done excellently, but you surpass them all."

Charm is deceitful, and beauty is vain, but a woman who fears the Lord is to be praised.

Give her of the fruit of her hands, and let her works praise her in the gates.

Some have mistakenly tried to paint her as a full-time career woman, yet this passage shows nothing of the kind. Some query that she was not always at home; she worked outside her home! Yes, she did. According to Scripture, she planted a vineyard in a field where she might have taken her children with her. I recall taking my children with me (when they were growing up) when gardening and farming. The Proverbs 31 woman also made linen garments for sale. I concur that this woman was not always at home, but the passage shows her focus was her home. Most of the things she did would allow her to work from home. Today, women can run successful businesses from home. I ran my confectionery business from home for decades before I moved into business premises. I even ran a poultry farm at home for years. Today, I know women who run successful day-care, write books, and run blog sites, who are accountants, telemarketers, and a host of other things from their homes.

Whether a Christian wife and mother should work outside the home depends on many factors. These include the ages of the children, the situation in the family, and God's leading. However, the Bible teaches the wife's priorities. If work causes a wife to neglect her family and home, then it is wrong for that woman to continue in that line of action. If a Christian mother can work and still provide a loving environment for her children and husband, then it is perfectly acceptable for her to do so. There is freedom in Christ. It is a fight of faith for Christians to live a life free from worldly expectations. We are free to live a modest lifestyle without compromising the comfort and special privileges of the family, free to accept God's validation over the world's, and free to do what is best for our precious families.

Women who work should not be condemned, neither should we treat women who focus on the stewardship of the home with condescension. In my experience, it is very possible for a wise Christian mother to work and still provide a loving environment. My mother did this all her life. Among the things needed to make this happen are a close walk with God, a rugged determination to work hard, organisation, flexibility, and diligence.

So, in considering 1 Timothy 5:11–15, Titus 2:3–5 and Proverbs 31:10–31, I could not agree more with Stephen Armstrong. I reiterate that:

- Homemaking is undeniably the mother's primary ministry, as given by God. While everyone in the family, including the husband, must share in the work of keeping a home, the woman is the chief homemaker.
- No Scripture prevents a wife or mother from seeking employment outside the home.
- If a married godly woman believes she can fulfil her biblical obligations in the home while also working outside the home, then she has liberty in Christ to do so. Each woman must decide what is best for her and her family, considering the counsel of the Holy Spirit and the Word of God.

My Personal Story as a Homemaker

In my first year after marriage and nine months after our first child was born, I worked full-time outside the home. As other children arrived, I studied for a master's degree, then worked from home full-time for five years. I returned to study part-time for a PhD degree for seven years before returning to part-time work and business. The point I want to make here is that all these years and even today, no matter how many hours I spend working outside of the home, part- or full-time, I have always considered myself a homemaker first. While the Bible gives no absolute restriction on where a woman may work, it provides a sense of priority. Most of the time I worked outside, my husband and I had to work as a team for our home to function properly. We worked hard and fast so we could still sit down and enjoy the evening together before bed. It was hard, especially after the children were born, I will be the first to admit. But that was just the way it had to be.

Being a homemaker also means that I cook, not because I am a slave to the kitchen, but because I love cooking. It is something I do for my family and myself. I like the time I have alone with my thoughts in the kitchen. I like the smell of jollof rice, beef/chicken stew, traditional African/continental cuisines, and baking bread/cake. But most of all, I love to sit down with my wonderful family, laugh and talk, and linger over a home-cooked meal at the end of the day. I love to hear my husband say, 'Darling, that was well cooked, thank you so much' and my children say, 'Mum, wow, you cook so well'. One of my children is still fond of saying, 'Mum, we are coming home, we cannot wait to devour your egg stew with fried yam and plantain'. I cannot describe my joy at hearing such wonderful comments from my family. They make cooking for them so delightful that I do not even consider it a chore.

Quite apart from cooking for my biological family, I love cooking for my church family and friends. I also rejoice and thank God for the wonderful comments that I hear from God's precious saints when I invite them home for a meal or cook for them after hosting meetings in my home. I am used to hosting and sometimes feeding over forty people in my home. That is a monumental job for some, but not for me. The joy I derive from cooking, watching God's people happy and enjoying themselves in my home, cancels the anxiety of hosting a crowd, tiredness, and fatigue.

Cleanliness is another core issue. The phrase 'Cleanliness is next to godliness' does not appear in the Bible. People credit its first use in English literature to the English philosopher and scientist Francis Bacon in 1605. He wrote, 'Cleanness of body was ever deemed to proceed from a due reverence to God'.

Almost two hundred years later (1791), a popular Anglican cleric and theologian, John Wesley, referred to the expression in one of his sermons in the form we use it today. Wesley wrote, 'Slovenliness is no part of religion. Cleanliness is indeed next to Godliness'.

Here is Wikipedia's definition and explanation of cleanliness:

Not to be confused with Cleanness or Cleaning. 'Cleanliness' is both the abstract state of being clean and free from germs, dirt, trash, or waste and the habit of achieving and maintaining that state. Cleanliness is often achieved through cleaning. Cleanliness is good quality, as indicated by the aphorism: 'Cleanliness is next to Godliness', and may be regarded as contributing to other ideals such as 'health' and 'beauty.'

Mark 7:5-7 states:

And the Pharisees and scribes kept asking [Jesus], Why do Your disciples not order their way of living according to the tradition handed down by the forefathers [to be observed], but eat with hands unwashed and ceremonially not purified? But He said to them, Excellently and truly so that there will be no room for blame] did Isaiah prophesy of you, the pretenders and hypocrites, as it stands written: These people [constantly] honor Me with their lips, but their hearts hold off and are far distant from Me. In vain (fruitlessly and without profit) do they worship Me, ordering and teaching [to be obeyed] as doctrines the commandments and precepts of men (Mark 7:5-7 AMPC).

Consider Jesus's words in the same chapter:

And He called the people to [Him] again and said to them, Listen to Me, all of you, and understand [what I say]. There is not [even] one thing outside a man which by going into him can pollute and defile him; but the things which come out of a man are what defile him and make him unhallowed and unclean (Mark 7:14-15 AMPC).

Outward cleanliness may appear to be unrelated to godliness. Jesus emphasised that handwashing should not be honoured more than the principle behind it. He never meant for religious leaders to use ceremonial law as justification for neglecting moral law. And he never intended for religious leaders to add fabricated traditions to burden people. Most of the instructions in the Torah and the Pentateuch—the Hebrew and Greek names, respectively, for the first five books of the Hebrew Bible, also known as the five books of Moses: (Genesis, Exodus, Leviticus, Numbers, and Deuteronomy)—can be compared to hygiene standards today. 'Cleanliness is next to godliness' is not explicitly stated in the Bible, but God wants His people to live in hygienic conditions.

When Husbands Do Their Fair Share of Housework

Many wives regard support from their husbands as a demonstration of love and appreciation. Overburdened wives may feel taken for granted and become dissatisfied with their marriage. It comes down to a simple point; when men do their share of domestic chores, the relationship benefits, but it suffers when either partner sees the split as unfair and unjustified. While housework may not directly lead to divorce, it is a backdoor that could disrupt a marriage. Bad feelings from any source, including housework, can spill over into other aspects of the relationship. Resentment affects how wives think and feel about their husbands, and that will come across in how they treat them.

Romeo Vitelli wrote an article titled *Is Doing Housework a Turn-On? New research on whether couples who share the load spend more time in bed.* This interesting article is about the study conducted by Matthew D. Johnson that was published in the Journal of Family Psychology, March 2016. According to his report, these researchers looked at the connection between male partner participation in housework and marital sex. They examined data from the Panel Analysis of Intimate Relationships and Family Dynamics (PAIRFAM) Study. This involved over 12,000 Germans born in 1971-73, 1981-83, and 1991-93.

All married participants completed questionnaires measuring aspects of marital life, sexual frequency, sharing housework, and whether the division was regarded as fair. Of the thousands of couples recruited for the larger study, they analysed couples who stayed together during the five stages of the study to see how their relationships grew and changed over time. On average, these couples had been together for nearly ten years, with 70 percent having one or more children.

Based on responses, couples enjoyed more frequent and satisfying sex when men contributed fairly to housework. This relationship between fair division of housework and sex held up remarkably well over time, despite other factors.

From the results, the actual amount of housework that men did was not as important in determining future sexual frequency as the cognizance that they did their fair share. Expectations about domestic chores often vary depending on the time men have available, how different cultures view men who do housework, and the relationship couples have.

The researchers' conclusions are remarkable:

Completing housework may or may not be enjoyable but knowing that a partner is pulling his weight prevents anger and bitterness, creating more fertile ground in which a (satisfying) sexual encounter may occur.

They also looked at female partner fairness and how it related to sexual frequency but found no sign of any actual link. Since we typically expect women to do their fair share of housework (if not more), men tend not to attach the same value to this as women do.

These findings and many others show how important it is that men pull their weight at home. Frequency of sex is not the only benefit that comes from sharing chores. Democratic couples also avoid relationship problems that often arise when one partner fails to do their bit. For couples seeking to stay together for the long run, establishing a real partnership, including fair division of household responsibilities, is more critical than you might think.

Being a homemaker is more than housekeeping. It is also about creating a place that is peaceful and inviting and comfortable in partnership with my husband. We work together as a team. I can say with Laura Hanby Hudgens:

But when it comes time to decorate, buy the throw cushions/pillows and the scented candles, that is all me. I hang the pictures of our family and tack their artwork on the wall when our children were young. I place reminders of our faith around the house. I grow my potted plants and put them and flower vases around the house. I make our house a home with comforts and small luxuries, through art, religious reminders, family keepsakes, and seasonal décor, not because these things by themselves are important, but because being a homemaker means creating a home that expresses who we are as a family. It means creating a place that feels like us.

I do not exclude my husband from any of the above activities—he is free to be involved.

There is more to being a homemaker than just what I do for my family in the home. I also manage most of the day-to-day business of family life. We often take food and snacks to gatherings. The children need gifts for birthday parties, our daughters need their hair fixed or an appointment with the doctor or dentist. When they were growing up, I managed most of that stuff. Even now that our children have left home, I am often required to travel to help with various things in their own homes, including babysitting. Why? Because I am the homemaker and know my priorities in my family.

I cherish the achievement of being a biomedical scientist, a PhD holder in medical and environmental microbiology, and an entrepreneur. This is my career and calling, and I am honoured and proud to be all of that. But they are not my primary occupation. My primary occupation remains homemaking, making a home for my husband and me, for our children to come home to, for our grandchildren to be spoiled in, and for God's people to be served. Being a homemaker is not just what I do. It is who I am and I love it! It is even more exciting and rewarding, doing it in partnership with my husband.

Tips for the Kingdom Homemaker

During my education, career, business, ministry, and in raising kids, God gave me powerful strategies to help cope as a homemaker. These include faith, running with His vision, diligence, prioritising, growing my confidence, and approaching life with courage and resilience. I learned that one can fall many times on their journey to fulfilling a dream and in life, but they can rise again.

No matter how many times you trip them up, God-loyal people don't stay down long; Soon they're up on their feet, while the wicked end up flat on their faces (Proverbs 24:16 MSG).

Fall seven times, stand up eight. You may encounter many defeats, but you must not be defeated. In fact, it may be necessary to encounter the defeats, so you can know who you are, what you can rise from.   —Maya Angelou

Serena Williams's version is also very inspiring and interesting:

I don't like to lose at anything. . . . Yet I have grown most not from victories, but setbacks. If winning is God's reward, then losing is how He teaches us; I really think a champion is defined not by their wins but how they can recover when they fall.

I am always inspired by certain Scriptures such as:

I can do all things [which He has called me to do] through Him who strengthens and empowers me [to fulfil His purpose—I am self-sufficient in Christ's sufficiency; I am ready for anything and equal to anything through Him who infuses me with inner strength and confident peace] (Philippians 4:13 AMP).

Make a careful exploration of who you are and the work you have been given, and then sink yourself into that. Don't be impressed with yourself. Don't compare yourself with others. Each of you must take responsibility for doing the creative best you can with your own life (Galatians 6:4-5 MSG).

Never give up on your dreams

I appreciate more today the reminders of God's help in the past. They reassure me that God's faithfulness continues and we can follow Him confidently into the future. The memories of what God has done becomes building blocks for trusting in what He will do. The Psalmist said:

> But then I recall all you have done, O Lord. I remember your wonderful deeds of long ago. They are constantly in my thoughts. I cannot stop thinking about your mighty works (Psalm 77:1-2 NLT).

I often encourage myself to relive victories, celebrate what God has done, and share my testimonies. Having developed the awareness of God's goodness, I keep saying; 'I know if God did it for me once, He will do it for me again'. When I missed my opportunity to go to medical school at 21, I promised myself that I would study for a PhD in medical sciences. It took 21 years. The journey was tough, and frequently, my studies came second to my family and other obligations. I finally completed my PhD programme in environmental and medical microbiology at Newcastle University Medical School after seven years of study. I am so grateful to God for making this dream a reality.

By God's grace, I have written and published two academic books, titled:

- *A Macro and Micro Study of the Environmental Impact of Sewage Discharges to Aquatic Environments Close Human Habitats*
- *Direct Viable Count Methods for Assessing Living Bacterial Numbers in Natural Waters.*

They showcase my research in medical and environmental microbiology and are still available on Amazon and eBay. I am so honoured that my books contribute to the ongoing 'Sanitary Revolution' (the introduction of clean water and sewage disposal) chosen by British Medical Journal (BMJ) readers as the most important medical milestone since the BMJ was first published. God gets all the glory!

I worked as a biomedical scientist, but later went freelance to suit my family commitments. I worked in various hospitals in the UK and overseas and somehow combined this with business. My confectionery business received a great boost after my local Government Council offered me premises at the Team Valley business centre in Gateshead, in the northeast of England. This helped me immensely, especially with flexibility to choose contracts at work. It also enabled me as an entrepreneur to interact with more people from different walks of life and build relationships with many Christian communities. I was elected the National Women's Coordinator of the Overseas Fellowship of Nigerian Christians (OFNC) UK in 2001 and served in this capacity for four years.

I passionately believe that marriage and the married life (lived out as God originally intended) can be one of the most rewarding experiences in this world. My husband and I often lead marriage seminars at various churches and conferences around the UK and abroad. Part of our vision is to empower couples with adequate resources and knowledge to help them make the best of their married lives. By God's grace, I am currently a trustee of three UK charities, the only wife of my loving husband, the mother of his children, and now a grandmother to God's glory.

Organising your home

Kingdom women should be organised. Becoming organised is a journey and not a destination. It takes time and patience. The key is to always keep pressing on. This is a decision you make every single day, even when you feel overwhelmed by the disarray of your home. All you can do sometimes may be to do one thing daily. Some days, you may feel you cannot get a single thing done. Ask God for His grace to do the next most important things.

Christian women are expected to look beautiful, dress gorgeously, and keep a lovely home. As a kingdom woman, when you embrace the homemaker role, you must be careful not to slip into materialistic understanding. Intentionally create a balance of personal and family wholesomeness. I am sure many hear that inward beauty counts. But more than hearsay, valuing the spiritual responsibility of character building is the essential core of homemaking. Character building is higher in value than the physical idea of housekeeping and needs to be taught more often.

Cooking and cleaning are chores some women delegate to others when necessary. One way to show your family love is by cooking their favourite meals. To me, family is the greatest gift God can give you after Jesus Christ. Therefore, seek to please God by choosing to be the best sister, wife, mother, and homemaker you could ever be.

While some women may see domestic chores as routine hard work best avoided at all costs, others see it as a special way of showing love for their family and pay tribute to Christ. Kingdom homemakers can take pleasure in their traditional roles as wives and mothers. If you would like to devote yourself to becoming a kingdom homemaker, there are several ways to go about it and I share some tips in this book.

The Challenge of Homemaking

Your homemaking career is important enough to demand your diligent preparation, foremost commitment, full energies, and greatest creativity. Doing this job without the enticement of a pay cheque requires understanding that what you do cannot be duplicated for any amount of money because you are 'worth far more than rubies' (Proverbs 31:10 NIV).

In Dorothy Patterson's article *The High Calling of Wife and Mother in Biblical Perspective*, she stated:

Dorothy Morrison wrote, 'Homemaking is not employment for slothful, unimaginative, incapable women. It has as much challenge and opportunity, success, and failure, growth, and expansion, perks, and incentives as any corporate career.'

....

ESSENTIAL POINTS FROM CHAPTER 3

- As the cliché goes, you can get the best out of any equipment or machinery by following the manufacturer's instruction, a condition necessary to keep the warranty. Since God instituted marriage and established the family, its ultimate success depends on following the instructions He has laid down.
- Like the Proverbs 31 woman, kingdom wives are to set the pace for excellence in partnership with their spouses. Kingdom husbands too must never think they are just *helping* their wives. Both work as a team for the benefit of the family.
- Godly homemaking is about building homes, where God's kingdom and grace can grow and flourish. Showing hospitality to all is one way of doing this.
- Kingdom women should feel confident in seeing homemaking as a wonderful career, a great privilege, ministry, and calling.
- A kingdom woman cannot be a panicky hysterical person because fear paralyses faith.
- We should not condemn kingdom women who work outside the home, part- or full-time. Neither should kingdom women who focus on the stewardship of the home be treated with condescension.

Declaration

I am a good and successful homemaker, a loving wife, and a doting mother. Like the Proverbs 31 woman, I observe the affairs of my household. I do not eat the bread of idleness and I am never lazy. By God's grace, I am strong, full of vigour and vitality. I am not a slave to my family or home. I am an excellent manager of my home. I organise my household in a way that helps things run smoothly. I spend my time doing what needs to be done. I do not waste time on activities that detract from the wellbeing of my family or from my faith. I am industrious and hardworking. I provide a pleasant and inviting atmosphere for everyone. I am beautiful, well dressed, and I take care of my body, which is the temple of the Most High God.

I declare this by faith in Jesus's majestic Name!

Further Study and Scripture References

Psalm 127; Proverbs 1:5, 3:5–6, 6:6–8, 10:4, 10:12, 12:24, 13:4, 13:16, 14:29, 17:17, 18:9, 24:27, 27:12; Matthew 25:14–30.

The Kingdom Woman as an Excellent Wife

Who can find a virtuous and capable wife? She is more precious than rubies (Proverbs 31:10 NLT).

Do nothing from selfish ambition or conceit, but in humility count others more significant than yourselves. Let each of you look not only to his own interests, but also to the interests of others (Philippians 2:3–4 ESV).

Who Is a Kingdom Wife?

Being a wife means a lot to me. I consider it a privilege, blessing, and special opportunity for service. I think God saw that Adam needed help, happiness, and fulfillment. He wanted to help the man; so, He channeled the help, favour, and grace into Eve and gave her to Adam. God probably could have done something else if He wanted. But in His great wisdom, He created the woman as the most valuable helpmeet for her husband—the one who complements him in every way and is a necessary part of his being.

And the Lord God said, it is not good that the man should be alone; I will make him an help meet for him (Genesis 2:18 KJV).

Then the Lord God said, 'it is not good for the man to be alone. I will make a helper who is just right for him' (Genesis 2:18 NLT).

For me, it was not just getting married. I wanted to be a godly wife of high quality and character. The first step any woman can take in that direction is to surrender to Christ. A kingdom wife believes in Jesus and has her priorities in order. She deliberately choses godliness as the focus of her life, and brings that focus into every relationship, especially marriage. This woman has decided that pleasing and obeying God is more important than her happiness. She is willing to make every sacrifice necessary to honour her Lord in her role as a wife.

If you are a Christian, you will agree that only in genuine surrender to the lordship of Christ can we see life from God's perspective, rather than our own agenda. That means that a Christian approaches marriage with a kingdom mindset. She desires to be a good wife to her husband and a godly woman for her Lord.

I like Tony Evans's quote that says, 'The Proverbs 31 woman is not necessarily a perfect woman but a transforming woman'.

By God's grace, I have been married for forty-three years. I can confidently say that marrying my darling husband, Dr. Nwachukwu James Nwabineli is the best decision I ever made after accepting Christ.

For many years, I looked up to my mum and other strong, godly women for inspiration. But the Proverbs 31 woman is an outstanding godly wife. This is the type of wife I always wanted to be, and by faith and the grace of God, I am becoming daily. Of course, I am far from perfect, but by fearing God and allowing the Holy Spirit to work within me, I am confident that I am growing all the time, and becoming a more mature, godly, and transforming wife. The indwelling Holy Spirit, who works to transform us from glory to glory can help us live godly lives (Galatians 2:20; Titus 2:12). Paul tells us what the Holy Spirit works out within us:

But the fruit of the Spirit is love, joy, peace, patience, kindness, goodness, faithfulness, gentleness, self-control; against such things there is no law (Galatians 5:22-23 ESV).

The Holy Spirit helps us develop His character. My prayer is that God would help me to be a woman who pursues Him daily. It takes courage, determination, and dependence on Him to intentionally grow and keep desiring growth in your marriage and every area. Phil Cooke writes, 'Growth is **what we do with knowledge**, how we apply it in our everyday lives'. It is a **never-ending process**—always learning, always moving forward, always achieving. Bob Gass stated:

> Look at the people in your circle of friends. Why do some succeed and others seem to stagnate? Why do some move to higher levels of achievement while others stay at the same place for years at a time? Many people blame the system, the company, or their boss. They blame society, their up-bringing, or their past. But a lifetime plan for growth can break through barriers and overcome nearly any obstacle.

The Bible puts it like this:

> The ways of right-living people glow with light; the longer they live, the brighter they shine. But the road of wrongdoing gets darker and darker—travelers can't see a thing; they fall flat on their faces (Proverbs 4:18-19 MSG).

Choose a mindset that you will please God first; remembering that He is the Originator and Designer of marriage. This opens the door for the miracles of God's intervention in your life and family. A basic characteristic of a godly wife is commitment to her husband. A kingdom woman should be faithful and dedicated to her husband. Her husband should be able to count on her unwavering support.

The kingdom wife should also be hardworking. She looks after her family responsibly, is resourceful, and applies her entrepreneurial skills in business. She takes care of herself and others. She is strong, dignified, confident, wise, and kind. These attributes gain her the respect of her husband and children.

While all the characteristics are valuable, **what sets a kingdom woman apart is the fear of God**. A wife should prioritise her husband over her children, but her top priority is God. Scripture shows marriage as a type of the relationship between the Church and Christ, and Paul tells us in Ephesians 5:21–30 what our attitudes and duties should be towards one another. Wise king Solomon writes:

> Her children arise and call her blessed; her husband also, and he praises her (Proverbs 31:28 NKJV).

I would say to husbands, if you have been too busy, self-absorbed, or distracted, change your ways. This equally applies to wives.

I grew up in a strong Roman Catholic tradition and the church had extremely strict teachings about marriage. This did not bother me at all as I did not contemplate marriage until many years later. A principle I discovered, which I teach women today, is that life flows uniquely through different seasons. Each season carries its own time-restraints, blessings, and distinctive demands. An awareness of seasons will help us to avoid failure or burnout in our pursuits.

A Woman's Identity Is Not Defined by Her Marital Status.

I want every woman reading to let this sink in; you and God are a powerful force to be reckoned with. You are an independent individual who can be successful in life regardless of your marital status. Some people believe that women are defined by men and their relationship to them. Not surprising that many women grow up dreaming of their wedding day and finding Mr Right as if their whole life purpose is to settle down with a man.

While marriage is a huge blessing and right for many reasons, it must never be viewed as the source of a woman's value and fulfilment. Only God can be that source. A wise Christian wife sees her role not as an end in itself, but as an avenue through which she can better serve her Lord (1 Corinthians 10:31). As one writer rightly said, some have exalted marriage as the ultimate goal, causing no small disillusionment. Many young women believe from childhood that, once they meet and marry the right man, they will be fulfilled. It is regrettable that much of the teaching we hear in the church today has contributed hugely to this exaltation of marriage. For an immature Christian woman, the disillusionment can feel as though God has deceived her.

While Christian mothers must continue to pray for and prepare their daughters for marriage, we must never imply that marriage is the ultimate goal. We should teach our daughters the value of their self-worth, among other things. There are three hallmarks of healthy self-esteem you should continually strive to teach your children: *Know who you are; Like who you are; Be who you are.* The fact is that some people have been chosen and graced by God to be single like Apostle Paul. There is nothing wrong with being single if that is God's will.

> I wish everyone could get along without marrying, just as I do. But we are not all the same. God gives some the gift of a husband or wife, and others he gives the gift of being able to stay happily unmarried. So, I say to those who aren't married and to widows— better to stay unmarried if you can, just as I am (1 Corinthians 7:7-8 TLB).

Apparently, Paul spent all but seven years of his ministry in prison, where he wrote the Epistles. His God-given assignment in life was suited to singleness. The point is, no one should ever be ashamed or embarrassed because he or she is single. Hear Bob Gass of blessed memory:

> Sometimes, when we see a woman or handsome man who is not married, we think, "I wonder what is wrong with them" Nothing! Indeed, something might be wrong with them if they married, because it is better to be single than to marry the wrong person.

However, there is everything wrong if it is God's will for you to get married and you do nothing about it and miss the opportunity.

Transitioning Roles: My Views as a Wife
(With My Husband Alone)

Over forty-three years of marriage, my views have changed as my role transitioned from being a wife to a wife and mother, to a wife, mother, and now grandmother. Our first child was born just thirteen months after we got married, so I did not spend a long time alone with my husband.

In that short period, I desired to be a godly woman and the perfect helpmeet for my husband. This entailed running to the cross of Christ and dying daily to myself. I learned how to lay down selfishness and put my plans aside. I had to drop my craving for recognition and focus on being a godly wife to a godly man. I was in love with my husband from the very beginning and, praise God, I still happily say *I do* every day, even after forty-three years. Over the years, God reveals my blind spots to me as I seek Him and strive to be the wife He created me to be. When I stand before God and recount my actions, attitudes, and overall role as wife to my husband, I would like the Lord to be happy with me. I would like to hear God say, 'Well done, good and faithful servant'.

> His master replied, 'Well done, good and faithful servant! You have been faithful with a few things; I will put you in charge of many things. Come and share your master's happiness' (Matthew 25:21 NIV).

Life is never devoid of challenges, but I have found God's grace is always more than sufficient for any Christian wife to perform her role selflessly and humbly. The irony is that being a godly wife does not mean pleasing my husband all the time. Of course, there is nothing wrong with that, within reason, as long as what pleases my husband does not go against God's will. But overall, I strongly believe I am called to perform my duties as a wife to glorify God first and be a walking representation of the Bride of Christ, the Church.

Ultimately, like every Christian, I am called to fear God in all I do (including my role as a wife). I have chosen to honour my God with my thoughts, words, and actions. Everything I have enjoyed in my entire life; I owe to God's grace. I, therefore, seek God's face and ask Him for the help I need in my decisions and actions. Instead of wasting time or comparing myself to others, I prefer to spend my time looking to the Shepherd and Bishop of my soul, asking Him to direct my path and develop me into His version of the Proverbs 31 woman.

As a disciple, living for Christ in your home is the acid test for your marriage. It is easier to live an excellent life in public, consciously putting your best foot forward, than to live for Christ indoors. You must remain true to who Christ is moulding you into. Never degenerate to a life repeatedly punctuated with bad temper, impatience, fault-finding, sarcasm, unkindness, suspicion, selfishness, or laziness. Instead, try to reveal through your daily life the fruit of the Spirit, which is love, joy, peace, and all the other virtues that reflect a Christ-like personality.

How to Fulfil Your Role as a Helpmeet

God created a helper for Adam, and this helper was suitable, fit, proper, and adapted for him. Through the years, the phrase *help meet* has transformed into a single word, *helpmeet*, sometimes used as a synonym for helpmate, spouse, or companion.

Modern translations render the phrase *helpmeet* as 'a helper fit for him' (ESV); 'a helper suitable for him' (NIV and NASB); or 'a helper comparable to him' (NKJV). **It is interesting to note that the only part of God's creation declared to be not good is Adam's solitary state.** Man is, by nature, a social creature; God created us to need companionship. And, of course, a man alone cannot propagate. Adam, by himself, was incomplete. This is the reason God created Eve to complete Adam, provide a society for him, and enable him to produce children. Eve was exactly what Adam needed.

So, what exactly does it mean to be a suitable helper? A suitable wife is compatible with her husband in many respects: physically, mentally, emotionally, and spiritually. This does not mean the man and woman are the same in everything, only that they fit together in harmony. They complement each other.

Nuggets to Help You Capture Your Husband's Heart

- Show your faith in God, clothed in humility, godly submission, and devotion.
- Once you are clear about God's will on anything, and you agree with your husband, follow through as He leads without hesitation. Be obedient to God's call.
- Be full of the Holy Spirit.
- Be a prayer warrior and pray for a discerning spirit.
- Be hospitable and have a passion for reaching the lost.
- Intentionally grow in your homemaking skills; study the many virtues of the Proverbs 31 woman.
- Develop resilience and willingness to sacrifice for your husband and children.
- Become committed to working hard for your family and invest in people.
- Let the fear of God make you beautiful inside and out. Never neglect your physical appearance; maintain physical attractiveness even as you grow in inner purity.
- Be determined to be the best cook; learn how to prepare your family's favourite meals.
- Love, respect, and honour your husband.
- Teach and show your children how to love and respect their dad.
- Love and honour your husband's family.
- Be the chief encourager of your husband in all God has assigned to him.

Consider this Scripture:

Do nothing from selfish ambition or conceit, but in humility count others more significant than yourselves. Let each of you look not only to his own interests but also to the interests of others (Philippians 2:3-4 ESV).

Being a kingdom wife involves living this out. Although it applies to all areas, I find it particularly helpful in eliminating most arguments with my husband. Humans are naturally selfish, so we must continually depend on the Lord to crucify our selfish urges and seek the best interest of others, giving priority to our spouses and children. For a kingdom wife, this means remaining conscious that her husband is also human and does not think like she does. The husband's needs differ from the wife's, and it is her responsibility to understand and seek to meet those needs whenever possible. This is also true for the husband.

The difference between an ordinary marriage and an extraordinary marriage is in a spouse's determination to give just a little extra every day as often as possible and for as long as they both shall live. Show me a man who is smiling from ear-to-ear and living a beautiful life, and I will show you a man who is grateful for what he has and utterly in love with his wife.

You do not base a happy marriage on how long you have been together. It is more about how much you love each other every day. This has been my experience for over forty-three years. Praise God, there is only one man I would marry repeatedly and that is the man in my life today, the man of my dreams, the godly, humble, and amazing father of our blessed children.

Let me share with you some life-changing lessons and observations from my marriage. Truth be told, women sometimes make wiser and smarter decisions than men, probably because of every woman's powerful sixth sense often referred to as a woman's instinct or intuition. Research has shown that women are more intuitive than men and can see blind spots that men may be oblivious to. A wife can get it wrong, especially when you think you need to be in charge because your husband would not lead.

I realise that sometimes my husband needs more time than I do to decide about things. I have also come to understand that men defer to logic and try to reason out things before deciding on a course of action. They, therefore, need more time.

I now know that men rarely show emotions the same way women do, and that they have a masculine perspective and approach life differently from women. I sincerely appreciate the fact that God designed women to complete and complement men.

Submission in Marriage

By God's grace, I have been training and counselling Christian couples, especially young ones, for many years. Starting from Benin City in Nigeria, where my husband and I led a group of couples in the church we attended, I was also privileged to co-lead the women's group. In Douglas, on the Isle of Man, I started the first women's group in the church my family attended and as previously mentioned was the Overseas Fellowship of Nigerian Christians (OFNC) national women's co-ordinator for four years.

My confectionery business is another powerful outlet the Lord has given me to minister to couples, especially engaged couples. I counsel and pray with many of them. As I design and craft wedding and celebration cakes, I pray over them. I also pray for the wedding ceremonies and marriages. Honestly, my cakes are not ordinary. I sanctify and load them with anointing and power to transform lives and marriages.

My husband and I have led marriage seminars at the OFNC national conferences, and in various churches at home and abroad. We still counsel couples. We have seen marriages restored and transformed by the power of God.

I recall counselling a handsome young Christian man who got entangled with the deceitfulness of the world and was confused about settling down. The Lord convicted him and cleaned up his life. He re-dedicated his life to God and got serious with a lovely Christian lady shortly after. To God's glory, today they are happily married with four children. I was at their wonderful wedding ceremony. In fact, I made their wedding cake.

I also recall four beautiful married Christian women I prayed for who could not conceive. They all became pregnant. God did what only Himself could do for these desperate daughters of His. I just rejoiced and blessed the Lord when one of them told me, 'Thank you very much auntie Betty for your prayers, but please stop praying for me since I now have four children and want no more'. Glory to God!

God has enabled my husband and I to become spiritual parents and grandparents to many. I believe God wants us to reproduce ourselves. He wants a return on His investment in our lives and marriage through our raising God-loving children.

One thing we have observed is that, although many couples are in love, they get caught up in major misunderstandings because of ignorance and manifestations of root sins like selfishness and pride. The reality is that a good marriage does not just happen. This truth cannot be overemphasised in the Body of Christ. You must work hard at it, just like anything else. For example, if you are a student, professional, businessperson, whatever you do, success is not automatic. You must work hard to become successful. Same with marriage! Marriage was God's idea, and His ideal of marriage is revealed in His Word. What you need to do is build your marriage according to God's instructions in His Word.

Therefore, be imitators of God as dear children. And walk in love, as Christ also has loved us and given Himself for us, an offering and a sacrifice to God for a sweet-smelling aroma (Ephesians 5:1–2 NKJV).

Wives, be *subject* to your own husbands, as [a service] to the Lord. For the husband is head of the wife, as Christ is head of the church, Himself *being* the Savior of the body. But as the church is subject to Christ, so also wives should be subject to their husbands in everything [respecting both their position as protector and their responsibility to God as head of the house].

Husbands, love your wives [seek the highest good for her and surround her with a caring, unselfish love], just as Christ also loved the church and gave Himself up for her, so that He might sanctify the church, having cleansed her by the washing of water with the word [of God], so that [in turn] He might present the church to Himself in glorious splendor, without spot or wrinkle or any such thing; but that she would be holy [set apart for God] and blameless. Even so husbands should *and* are morally obligated to love their own wives as [being in a sense] their own bodies. He who loves his own wife loves himself. For no one ever hated his own body, but [instead] he nourishes *and* protects and cherishes it, just as Christ does the church, because we are members (parts) of His body. For this reason a man shall leave his father and his mother

87

and shall be joined [and be faithfully devoted] to his wife, and the two shall become one flesh. This mystery [of two becoming one] is great; but I am speaking with reference to [the relationship of] Christ and the church. However, each man among you [without exception] is to love his wife as his very own self [with behavior worthy of respect and esteem, always seeking the best for her with an attitude of lovingkindness], and the wife [must see to it] that she respects *and* delights in her husband [that she notices him and prefers him and treats him with loving concern, treasuring him, honoring him, and holding him dear] (Ephesians 5:21–33 AMP).

These are some passages many refer to when talking about marriage. In Ephesians 5:22–24, Paul instructs wives to submit to their husbands. Immediately before this, **he instructs the whole church at Ephesus to submit to one another.** Then, he moves onto the marriage relationship. It is unfortunate that some Christians take these verses and make them say something they do not say, making a wife feel inferior to her husband.

Many wives today struggle with the word *submit*. When these verses are taken out of context and applied to women only, they become tools in the devil's hand. The enemy often twists the Word of God to accomplish his evil purposes and has used this to do a lot of damage to God's beautiful plan for marriage.

Referring to some full gospel preachers, Pa Kenneth Hagin stated:

They insist that wives must submit themselves to their husbands in all things as unto the Lord. They leave the impression that the man is the dictator of the home and the woman is supposed to do whatever the man says. That implies that we in the Church are also supposed to be dictators over one another, because verse 21 tells the whole church at Ephesus, 'Submit yourselves to one another.' We all know what the result would be—total chaos in the Church.

I reiterate that Apostle Paul was talking to the whole church in verse 21. He did not intend Christians to lord it over one another. What he was saying is that we are to give in, and be agreeable, pleasant, and get along with one another. Then, the next verse does not mean the husband is to lord it over his wife, that she is never to have any say. Far from it! There is no doubt this verse applies to wives, but it places the bulk of the responsibility upon the husband to love his wife the way Christ loves the church (Ephesians 5:25–32). It also means that the husband and wife are to be agreeable and endeavour to get along with each other. The bottom line is that when a husband lives in obedience to God's expectation for him, a wife has little difficulty submitting to his leadership.

Another passage often referred to about submission is 1 Peter 3:1–7. The New Testament Greek word translated into English as *submit (yourselves)* is *hupotasso*. It is used in 1 Peter 3:1 and elsewhere regarding Christians submitting to one another.

Besides studying God's Word, I thoroughly researched this topic on submission, and here is an interesting and powerful excerpt from *The Woman Question* by late Pa Kenneth E. Hagin. He had a massive understanding and revelation about this subject. On pages 19 and 24, he wrote:

> But as a wife, in the natural human relationship, she has a subordinate place in the family. (She does not have a subordinate place in the body of Christ. And this does not mean that husband and wife are not equal before God.) For the sake of good order in the family, the husband should be the head of the house. No intelligent woman should think of marrying a man who in her estimation is not worthy to take that place.
>
> Great calamities might have been averted if God's order in family government had been accepted and followed. The husband is not to be contrary and lord it over his wife. Rather they are to be helpers together in all which concerns their temporal and eternal welfare.
>
> The husband must carry the greater responsibility, therefore he should have the higher authority. If both husband and wife are what they should be, the husband will take his place naturally as the head of the family, and it will be a joy to his wife to see him there. No real woman wants a mere echo or a puppet for a husband. It should be the wife's delight to submit her will to her hus-

band's when necessary, rather than make him the laughingstock of his neighbours. There is no escape from the plain teaching of the Word of God on this point.

Women are not subordinate to men. It is a husband-and-wife proposition. Wives do have a subordinate place in the family. They do not have a subordinate place in the Lord. The Bible says, ". . . there is neither male nor female: for ye are all one in Christ Jesus" Galatians 3:28. **Women are called "sons of God" just as much as men are. John was writing to the entire church—not just to the men—when he said,** "Beloved, now are we the sons of God. . . ." (1 John 3:2). That verse continues, ". . . and it doth not yet appear what we shall be: but we know that, when he shall appear, we shall be like him; for we shall see him as he is." Women will be like Him just as much as men will be (emphasis mine).

Another Scripture that the devil often twists to corrupt God's plan for Christian marriages is:

Like Sarah who obeyed Abraham and called him her lord. You are her daughters if you what is right and do not give way to fear (1 Peter 3:6 NIV).

Peter refers to Sarah (the first of the four matriarchs of the Jewish nation and widely referred to as Sarah *Imeinu*, Sarah Our Mother), a model wife whose worthy example Christian wives should emulate. It is easy for a Christian husband to take this verse out of context and insists that his wife obeys him and calls him lord like Sarah did. Yes, a wife should obey her husband, but it does not mean that the wife does not have a right to make her point. Some create the impression the wife cannot express her thoughts, that she is under the rule and domination of her husband and is almost a slave.

I like the account of Sarai in Genesis 16. Verses 5 and 6 show how Abram allowed Sarai to have her way. Here, for whatever reason, God justified Sarai, not Abram. Genesis 21:10-12 records another account where God specifically told Abram to listen to Sarai. On this occasion,

God approved of her decision, as He always does when a wife is right. God always approves of right. When Sarah was right, God sided with her. God will never take sides with the husband when he is wrong, any more than He will side with the wife when she is wrong.

Pa Hagin once shared how some Spirit-filled, Full Gospel ministers told him that a woman ought to do whatever her husband says, no matter what. They told him in person that if the husband tells his wife to drink with him, she ought to drink with him. If he wants her to go to the bar, she should go. If a husband tells his wife not to go to church, she is not to go. If he tells her not to read the Bible, she is not to read it. She is to obey him to the letter. I could not agree with Pa Hagin more that God will never side with wrong since that would violate His commandments. Misinterpreting God's Word causes a lot of confusion in the body of Christ. In Pa Hagin's words on page 27 of his book:

> Thank God for good wives! They don't need to be put down. Oh, I know there are some bossy wives, but if their husbands don't know how to take care of them, let them go ahead and be henpecked. You see, it is the husband's problem. There's no use in downgrading all wives because of a few exceptions. And it is the responsibility of the husbands to take care of that—not the responsibility of the preachers. If a man wants to be henpecked, it's his business, and no one else's. I have no more business trying to manage another man's wife than I have managing some other fellow's money. We can lay down principles, of course. But I think there are some men who rather enjoy being henpecked. If they do—let them enjoy it. I don't like it myself.

I am impressed by the fact that our first mother Sarah did not suffer in silence and servile subjection but spoke her mind as she had a right to do (See Genesis 16:5, 6). 1 Samuel 1:23 records that Hannah spoke her mind and had her way regarding Samuel. It proved to be God's way.

Abigail, as you will see later, was a wise woman whose husband was called a 'son of Belial'. By disobeying her husband, Abigail saved a critical situation and won the favour of David. If she had listened to her foolish husband, there would have been much bloodshed. Let us consider David's response to Abigail in the following Scripture:

> Then David said to Abigail, blessed be the Lord God of Israel, who sent you this day to meet me, and blessed be your discernment, and blessed be you, who have kept me this day from bloodshed and from avenging myself by my own hand. Nevertheless, as the Lord God of Israel lives, who has restrained me from harming you, unless you had come quickly to meet me, surely there would not have been left to Nabal until the morning light as much as one male (1 Samuel 25:32–34 NASB).

It is obvious from the rest of the story that God sided with Abigail, even though she disobeyed her husband. Like Pa Hagin, I believe it is an unreasonable argument that every wife must obey her husband in everything. As kingdom people, we must always consider the teachings of the entire Bible. We are not to take an isolated text and build some doctrine on it.

I refer to Pa Kenneth Hagin again. On page 30 of his book, he stated:

> If an enraged husband commanded his wife to kill their children, no sane person would say she should obey. Well, if she shouldn't obey that, there are a lot of other things she shouldn't obey—because they are wrong! A HUSBAND CANNOT COUNTERMAND ANY OF THE LORD'S COMMANDMENTS.

Marg Mowczko stated:

> I think much of the church has a faulty idea of submission in marriage. Biblical submission is not about blind obedience or subservience. Healthy submission is characterised by loyalty, humility, and consideration, and it seeks the greater good. Ideally, it should be mutual and reciprocal, rather than one-sided, with both husband and wife helping and serving each other.

Walk in Love

Husbands, love your wives, just as Christ also loved the church and gave Himself for her (Ephesians 5:25 NKJV).

This kind of love is not carnal and far exceeds human love. It is a kind of love where the husband puts his wife first and loves her better than he does himself. And she of course, also loves him with God's divine love.

Communication in Marriage

Communication is crucial for harmony. Sometimes, husbands must be reminded to do the obvious at home. To avoid unnecessary arguments and strife, a wife should initiate non-judgmental conversations with her husband, explaining how he can help and what she needs from him to be more responsive to his needs. In my experience, couples who stay connected and set aside **intentional times together** grow stronger and build deeper bonds that will keep their marriage healthy.

A pragmatic wife also realises that it is right and not selfish to take time to look after herself. She is honest with her husband about her own mental, emotional, physical, and psychological needs. Wives who neglect or fail to express their own needs for fear of appearing selfish are only setting themselves up for resentment and burnout. Before a wife and mother can give her family members what they need, she must take care of herself.

There are two model wives in the Bible that have inspired me the most. The first is Sarah and the second is Abigail. I am motivated by Sarah's love and submission as she left all she had ever known and went with Abraham to an undetermined place and an uncertain future, commanded by an unknown God. When God called Abram to move in Genesis 12:1–6, Sarai moved, too. Someone might ask: was she expected to marry and not relocate with her husband? If she did not, the marriage would crash. Think about that.

Sarai left everything she had to migrate with her husband to a land they had never seen and knew nothing about. They trusted and completely depended on God. They must have wondered about this God! Who is this unknown God? Can He be trusted? Could He deliver on His promises? Is He a good, generous, and holy God? In Genesis 15, at a place called Haran, the only true God suddenly revealed Himself to Abraham.

> He also said to him, 'I am Yahweh who brought you from Ur of the Chaldeans to give you this land to possess' (Genesis 15:7 HCSB).

Like all of us, Sarah must have had her flaws, but her character intrigues me. She is even mentioned among the heroes of faith:

> Because of faith also Sarah herself received physical power to conceive a child, even when she was long past the age for it because she considered [God] Who had given her the promise to be reliable and trustworthy and true to His word (Hebrews 11:11 AMPC).

I admire Sarah as an excellent wife, whose virtues I endeavour to emulate.

> We want each of you to show this same diligence to the very end so that what you hope for may be fully realized. We do not want you to become lazy, but to imitate those who through faith and patience inherit what has been promised (Hebrews 6:11-12 NIV).

There is power in imitation and the writer encourages us to emulate those who have found the key to gaining God's promises. Abraham and Sarah showed the two keys of faith and patience in very profound ways. They had some weaknesses, but their faith in God received the highest commendation. Hence, Abraham is called the father of faith. When I think about Sarah's faith and patience, they spur my determination to overcome discouragement and to keep fighting every day. It helps me never give up.

My Inspiration from Sarah's Life

Sarah reminds me of how I also left everything I had after I got married. I had an amazing job as a Research Scientist, a beautiful car, and an ambition to earn a PhD, just to mention a few. But my resolve was tested less than a year after our wedding. My husband had to relocate to the United Kingdom to specialise as an Obstetrician and Gynaecologist. That meant I had to give up my job, car, and academic goal. I had to defer everything to support him. I desired to see my husband reach the zenith of his career as one of the best Obstetricians and Gynaecologists of his time. Today, I can confidently say to God's glory, this has come to pass.

I was twenty-one years old when I purposed to study for a PhD programme, but it was another twenty-one years before it happened. When I finally started the programme as a mature student of forty-two, it took seven years to get my PhD. My studies took longer because once I started, I would not allow it to adversely affect my husband's career, our children's education, or the harmony and tranquillity in our home. I happily suspended my studies when it was not convenient for the family. I moved towns, cities, and changed countries with my husband to see him succeed and excel in his career and he has always remained so appreciative of my sacrifice. God gets ALL the glory.

Sometimes, I emulate Sarah so much that I draw parallels in my mind between her journey and mine. Abraham married well. He loved this beauty of a woman named Sarah. God helped my husband choose his beautiful wife called Betty. God changed her name from Sarai to Sarah, meaning *princess*. My name was also changed from Ophiame to Ivie meaning *precious*. I have been inspired by the way she maintained herself and nurtured her God-given dream. Likewise, I strive to keep fit and healthy as I age gracefully. I continue to be inspired by her faith in God.

Many passages in the Bible exhort Christians to live by faith.

For, 'In just a little while, he who is coming will come and will not delay.' And, 'But my righteous one will live by faith. And I take no pleasure in the one who shrinks back' (Hebrews 10:37-38 NIV).

Faith was the key that empowered Sarah to maintain her dream. I can recall how overly concerned some well-meaning friends were when I left university without a boyfriend. I knew that God who gave me the desire to marry would provide His own man for me at the appointed time. Miraculously, I met my amazing husband during National Youth Service Corps (NYSC) in Kano, Nigeria. It has been a blissful and fruitful forty-three years and it gets better daily by God's grace.

Sarah's fight of faith has inspired my journey of faith in many ways

- Raising my family, studying, and doing scientific research at the same time was physically demanding and arduous.
- Waiting twenty-one years to start my dream of completing a PhD programme was not easy. I could have given up and made valid excuses, but like Sarah, I pressed on.
- When I lost both parents within six months and was suddenly left to be the mother of several younger siblings, all I had left was faith in God. It was the only thing that kept me going when I worked so many jobs to make ends meet in Nigeria.
- Each time I started my business in the UK and Nigeria, it took courage and faith in God to start, to keep going, and to succeed.
- When I travelled the world as a freelance biomedical scientist, it took faith to execute each contract excellently and still be a homemaker.
- It took faith in God to remain calm and immovable when my family was served two deportation notices and warned not to settle in the British Isles. Details later, but by God's grace, not long after, we were made British citizens.
- When my husband finally finished his specialist training in the UK, it took faith in God to overcome a health challenge. He suddenly developed bilateral retinal detachment in both eyes just four months after we returned to Nigeria. Some of his colleagues thought it was the end of his medical career, but God healed both eyes miraculously and he never had a relapse. We give all the glory

to God. We have fought other health battles in the family, and God has come through for us every time.

· There was an attempt by detractors to have my name struck off the professional register and my license to practice as a biomedical scientist in the United Kingdom revoked. It is one of the greatest miracles/breakthroughs I received from God in the UK because God disgraced my accusers and vindicated me. This is a huge testimony for another book.

· To reach my goals in Christ and life, I have learned to push through public opinion and intimidation. I have tasted the bitter flavour of fear and pressed on with faith in God when nothing else seemed to make sense. Frequently, I had to confront difficult issues, face my fears, and survive the stares of my peers who did not fully understand who I was then.

I also learned a lot from Sarah's love for her son, Isaac. I like the determination with which she fought for Isaac's inheritance. Sarah's jealousy for Isaac as their only heir complemented God's design and promise to Abraham and Sarah:

> But God said to Abraham: 'Do not be distressed because of the lad and your maid; whatever Sarah tells you, listen to her, for through Isaac your descendants shall be named' (Genesis 21:12 NASB).

> It was he to whom it was said, 'In Isaac, your descendants shall be called.' He considered that God can raise people even from the dead, from which he also received him back as a type (Hebrews 11:18-19 NASB).

Sarah knew what she was doing. She understood God's promise, protected her son, and defended her household from a polygamous relationship. She remained faithful in her marriage through thick and thin. Her virtues are unchallenged as an example for women and men forever, and that inspires me.

Do not let your adorning be external—the braiding of hair and the putting on of gold jewelry, or the clothing you wear—but let your adorning be the hidden person of the heart with the imperishable beauty of a gentle and quiet spirit, which in God's sight is very precious. For this is how the holy women who hoped in God used to adorn themselves, by submitting to their husbands, as Sarah obeyed Abraham, calling him lord. And you are her children if you do good and do not fear anything frightening (1 Peter 3:3–6 ESV).

We also read about the virtuous woman:

Her husband is known in the gates when he sits among the elders of the land (Proverbs 31:23 ESV).

Have you ever wondered why this one sentence in the middle of a lengthy description of the woman? I guess the writer knew a timeless secret that many people in our modern world seem to forget—**a woman has a tremendous impact on her husband's success.** I emulate this admirable virtue from Sarah and the Proverbs 31 woman. I have therefore resolved to be the greatest inspiration for my husband, like no one else in his life. I purposefully help, encourage, and call forth his gifts.

A woman's words can be mighty, so I continue to depend on God to help me choose mine carefully as I speak health, victory, love, and life into my husband, children, and grandchildren. By God's grace, today my wonderful children arise and call me blessed, and I have also gained the praise of my husband according to Proverbs 31:28. My prayer is that I will continue to grow and abound more and more in love and the fear of the Lord in Jesus's mighty name.

As a wife, I am highly influenced by how Sarah transcended the occasional apprehensions of married life. Couples may have different perspectives based on reason and intuition, so a wife can become apprehensive of her husband's decisions. This is where good communication comes into play. I believe Sarah and Abraham had good communication in their marriage, and that helped her look to God.

I know that men rarely show emotions the same way women do. They have a masculine perspective that makes them approach life differently. Now, I realise that God designed women to complete and complement men. I deliberately give my husband space to think and process his ideas. I had to study the way he thinks, understand what real masculinity is, and embrace it—instead of trying to make him more feminine. The differences between men and women are very important, and God can use them for the greater good. But we must look at our husbands' strengths and appreciate the way God designed them instead of trying to make them think and feel like we do.

I am forever inspired by Sarah's faith

Over the years, I realised that my husband cannot meet all my needs. Only God can. Therefore, I must look to God. My husband cannot become God to me. Putting him in God's place will equate to idolatry. Only God can be God to me. Should my husband fail me in any way, I remain unshaken because my heart is set on Christ, my King and Lord, not my husband. I have experienced how God gives supernatural strength, wisdom, peace, and even joy to handle difficulties when I abide in and seek Him first with all my heart, mind, soul, and strength.

Although God had given His word, Sarah and Abraham tried to work things out their way. Sarah attempted to improve on God's timetable, with dire consequences. Rather than waiting on God, since they were quite old, they decided to help God. They had to learn the difference between human effort and faith. But they received God's truth with humility and readiness to act on what they heard.

They were convicted (which is more than being merely convinced) of God's instruction. This all translated into strong faith. Sarah waited on God and 'judged Him faithful who had promised' (Hebrews 11:11 KJV). The entire miraculous event was reduced to patient waiting on God to answer—which I find very encouraging.

Moses shows how Sarah's laughter changed:

And the Lord visited Sarah as He had said, and the Lord did for Sarah as He had spoken. For Sarah conceived and bore Abraham a son in his old age. . . . And Sarah said, 'God has made me laugh ['made laughter for me' or 'granted me the ability to laugh and rejoice'], and all who hear will laugh [and rejoice] with me' (Genesis 21:1–6 KJV).

I love this. It is surely my testimony.

Originally, Sarah laughed at the ridiculousness of a ninety-year-old having a child. But after she gave birth to Isaac, her sceptical laughter changed to pure joy. Now she enjoyed the laughter of faith. What satisfaction she must have felt, what peace and comfort. Sarah's remarkable example is in Hebrews 11, which recounts many inspiring stories of faith. Peter rightly commends all faithful women of all ages when he wrote:

> As Sarah obeyed Abraham, calling him lord, whose daughters you are if you do good and are not afraid ... (1 Peter 3:6 NKJV).

The implication is clear. Sarah is a shining example of the practice of faith for all Christian women. By God's grace, like Sarah, I enjoy the laughter of faith.

Abigail: A Woman with Beauty and Brains

Abigail, although a lesser-known heroine has also inspired me. Marg Mowczko describes her as 'A Bible woman with beauty and brains'.

Her name, derived from two Hebrew words, means *my father's happiness* or *father's joy*. She may have been the cause of happiness in her father's house.

The story of how she met David and eventually became his wife is fascinating. I learned a lot from this Old Testament woman of faith.

Her story is found in 1 Samuel 25. Scripture gives no clue as to her parentage or genealogy, nor does it tell us how Abigail first got married. This amazing woman is described as *intelligent* (NAB, NIV, CEV), *clever* (NRSV), and of *good understanding* (KJV, ASV). As the wife of a rich man, she enjoyed the benefits of an affluent lifestyle and a high socioeconomic status. Unfortunately, her husband was a scoundrel. Nabal's name means *foolish* or *senseless*.

Now the name of the man was Nabal, and the name of his wife Abigail. The woman was discerning and beautiful, but the man was harsh and badly behaved; he was a Calebite (1 Samuel 25:3 ESV).

The contrast is visible in their names and attitudes. Nabal's character is precisely like his name, foolish. Abigail, on the other hand, was wise and intelligent. Phyllis Bird (one translator of the New Revised Standard Version of the Bible) describes Abigail as:

Intelligent, beautiful, discreet and loyal to her husband (despite his stupidity and boorish character). Prudent, quick-witted, and resourceful, she is capable of independent action.

While Nabal is the proverbial fool, Abigail epitomizes the wife of noble character. One might wonder why such an incredible woman would marry a fool! Abigail should take no blame for this because it is likely her parents arranged her marriage as was prevalent in their culture. We cannot overlook Abigail's unmistakably complementary description contrasted with Nabal's derogatory epithet. Nabal is introduced in terms of his possessions (what he had) while Abigail is introduced in terms of her character (who she was). Her person preceded her possessions. This underlines the fact that who you are is more important than what you have.

Abigail's wise response to an imminent threat

What did Abigail do when she heard about David's vengeful plans to exterminate Nabal's household?

1. She **quickly** prepared a feast for David and his men. She **secretly** prepared to meet him with a gift. Consider 1 Samuel 25:18a:

   Abigail acted **quickly** (NIV).
   Abigail wasted **no time** (NLT).
   Then Abigail **made haste** (AMPC) (emphasis mine).

Abigail then rides out to meet David with an apology that sets a new standard for courtesy. She fell on her face before David and took complete responsibility for the cruel decision and actions of her husband. She immediately postured herself as a servant to David. Notice she addressed David as 'my lord' at least ten times in her speech while addressing herself six times as his servant (1 Samuel 25:24–31 NIV). Consider the gracious words with which she conveyed hard truths David needed to hear. This anointed king-in-waiting is on the verge of needless bloodshed, bringing on himself a guilt he could never escape. I love the wisdom she displayed as she made a very personal and powerful appeal to David.

2. She did not let Nabal know her plans. Wise Abigail, the invisible guard, acted with wisdom behind the scenes. No talking about it and ruining her husband's image in front of people. She just quietly went about what she had to do.

For thus said the Lord Jehovah, the Holy One of Israel, in returning and rest shall ye be saved; in quietness and in confidence shall be your strength (Isaiah 30:15 ASV).

David's response

Abigail's words moved David, and he abandoned his revenge agenda. He even thanked Abigail for diverting him from his reckless plan. David recognised Abigail as an angel of God. If Abigail had not intercepted him, she would have been caught up in the massacre.

Lessons to Learn from Abigail's Story

This incredible woman was married to a difficult, evil man. Her challenge was to live peaceably with her harsh and unkind husband while preserving her own integrity and strength of character. That required discretion in her words and actions to achieve the best outcome. The Bible admonishes godly women to be discreet.

To be discreet, chaste, keepers at home, good, obedient to their own husbands, that the word of God be not blasphemed (Titus 2:5 KJV).

Dictionary.com defines discretion as 'the quality of behaving or speaking in such a way as to avoid causing offense or revealing private information; and the freedom to decide what should be done in a particular situation'.

Discretion could require acting quickly

Abigail instantly perceived the enormity of the situation and acted without hesitation. Wisdom and resolve may need to partner to prevent disaster. **Being wise in itself may not be sufficient in some situations. You must take immediate action, instead of simply standing by to watch destruction that could have been averted. An astute, godly woman is proactive and prompt to act.** Abigail's quick thinking, deliberate action, and diplomatic speech saved many lives.

Abigail was a prudent and God-fearing woman

I believe Abigail feared and walked with God. She respected David as the future king. Besides, it would take a God-fearing woman empowered and led by the Holy Spirit to live successfully with a husband like Nabal and yet conduct herself the way Abigail did. Hear her:

> 'When God completes all the goodness he has promised my master and sets you up as prince over Israel, my master will not have this dead weight in his heart, the guilt of an avenging murder. And when God has worked things for good for my master, remember me' (1 Samuel 25:30–31 MSG).

David's response is profound:

'Blessed be God, the God of Israel. He sent you to meet me! And blessed be your good sense! Bless you for keeping me from murder and taking charge of looking out for me. A close call! As God lives, the God of Israel who kept me from hurting you, if you had not come as quickly as you did, stopping me in my tracks, by morning there would have been nothing left of Nabal but dead meat' (1 Samuel 25:32–34 MSG).

Fellowship with the Holy Spirit enables us to know His mind and do as He leads. A godly woman who continually walks in the Spirit is one who prays without ceasing because she is constantly communing with the Holy Spirit. She enjoys His unfailing presence with her all the time. He is her Helper, Advocate, Standby, and Counsellor.

Abigail did not need to pray endlessly for God's leading on the matter. I believe she was in constant communion with God. It appears that Abigail, by the amazing character she displayed, may have been one of the few in Old Testament times who, like king David in Psalm 51:10–12; Joshua in Numbers 27:18; Othniel in Judges 3:10, and Bezaleel in Exodus 31:1–3, received the Holy Spirit before it was given more generally in New Testament times. Hence, when she needed to make a decision without delay, the God she knew was standing by her to guide her in what to do. She acted immediately as she was guided by her Helper, saving her entire household.

Sometimes discretion hinges on courage and faith

Abigail was a courageous woman who made the best of a difficult situation. A small lone figure, riding a donkey straight into a troop of 400 armed men bent on revenge. That required great courage and faith. The Lord honoured Abigail for her consistency, generosity, and willingness to continue on the right path, no matter how difficult. In the same way, God honours those who are faithful through hardship and pain. He does not promise to always deliver, as he delivered Abigail, but He promises to go with us.

As mothers endowed with the awesome responsibility of raising the next generation for Christ, there are many situations in life that require courage. Discretion and wisdom are often required to determine the best course of action. Nabal's foolishness had grave ramifications, but Abigail realised that, given the circumstances, she was the only one who might avert impending disaster and preserve her household. This is a crucial lesson for mothers to learn.

Sometimes discretion hinges on proper timing

Abigail arrived home to find her husband throwing a party and getting drunk. The Bible says she did not tell him anything about her activities then. She would not hide anything from him, but timing was important. Abigail may have expected repercussions when she confessed what she had done. But there was an unexpected outcome.

> In the morning, when the wine had gone out of Nabal, his wife told him these things, and his heart died within him, and he became as a stone. And about ten days later the Lord struck Nabal, and he died (1 Samuel 25:37-38 ESV).

A timeless example

Abigail's quick thinking, courage, discreet words, and faith in God saved lives. When David later married her, she likely served as a constant reminder to the future king of Israel of the value of discretion. She surely does to me and all those reading her story.

Abigail's humility

Abigail's humility silenced her enemy and completely changed David's response to the situation. David even apologised to Abigail and thanked her for her words that restrained him from killing many innocent people in his anger (verses 32–34). Then David's men received all the provisions she had provided.

> Likewise you younger people, submit yourselves to your elders. **Yes, all of you be submissive to one another, and be clothed with humility, for 'God resists the proud, But gives grace to the humble'** (1 Peter 5:5 NKJV) (emphasis mine).

In Abigail, we witness a woman who remained humble before her enemies, even someone who had the power to destroy her life and family. Abigail could have adopted a bad attitude toward David, but through her humility, one of her greatest strengths, she saved her entire household. And because her heart was right even toward her harsh husband, God honoured her and positioned her to become a queen. In Denise Renner's words, 'A humble position is a powerful position! Abigail's story is amazing, and we can learn a lot from her.'

She also said that even though Abigail was a rich woman, she remained humble. Abigail did not set her heart on her wealth. She risked everything to save her household. Through the years, as she humbled herself before her cruel husband time and time again, God was building character within her heart, causing her to grow into a respectful and powerful woman, even during adversity. I agree with Denise Renner that Abigail did not nag her husband, even though she had the right to say, *Wise up now, everyone knows that you are a fool! Your foolishness is going to get everyone killed in our home! I have told you several times to do something about your evil ways.*

An attitude of humility, honour and respect gives a person boldness. Humble, honouring, and respectful people believe for God's good plan and keep expecting the best outcome. Abigail was forgiving. Her exemplary life illustrates that humility, honour, respect, and wisdom do not mix with bitterness and unforgiveness.

Abigail did not repay evil for evil

Abigail was thinking about her enemies' good when she faced David and his men. Jesus said:

> Bless those who curse you, and pray for those who spitefully use you (Luke 6:28 NKJV).

Abigail knew David and his troops needed food. She focused on their need, not their anger and threats. I could not agree more with Denise Renner that the attitude of most people would be to give them a piece of her mind! But we can see through Abigail's example that even while living under the cruel hand of her spouse, **God was putting the attributes of a queen into her.**

I am so impressed that this honourable woman did not leave her ungodly husband or seek divorce, but remained a loyal wife and protector of her worthless spouse. That is a huge credit to her. As far as she was concerned, she had taken him for life. One can only imagine how miserable Abigail's life would have been, especially during Nabal's drinking bouts. Even then, she clung to the man to whom she had sworn to be committed. Abigail manifested a love stronger than death.

> Beloved, never avenge yourselves, but leave it to the wrath of God, for it is written, 'Vengeance is mine, I will repay, says the Lord' (Romans 12:19 ESV).

Christians often take vengeance into their own hands. The entire world is in chaos today. People in conflict could learn a valuable lesson from this wise and courageous peace-loving woman, Abigail, whose story is almost like an illustration of this verse.

Abigail was a woman of poise

In Mackintosh W. Mackay's classic book titled, *The Woman of Tact, and Other Bible Types of Modern Women*, he wrote concerning Abigail:

She possessed in harmonious combination these two qualities which are valuable to any one, but which are essential to one who has to manage men—*the tact of a wise wife and the religious principle of a good woman.*

An article on LovingGod.com website stated:

Eugenia Price, who writes of Abigail as, *A Woman With God's Own Poise,* says that, "only God can give a woman poise like Abigail possessed, and God can only do it when a woman is willing to co-operate as Abigail cooperated with Him on every point." True to the significance of her own name she experienced that in God her Father there was a source of joy enabling her to be independent of the adverse, trying circumstances of her miserable home life.

Abigail was a peacemaker

Jerome Blanco wrote:'We live in a world of Nabals and Davids. Sometimes, if we're honest, we take up their roles ourselves. People harm people, on personal levels, on organizational levels, on societal levels. It isn't hard to find situations that ache for peacemaking. (A quick scroll through the web's headlines and comment sections can tell anyone that.) When there is wickedness, what does acting urgently and wisely for the sake of peace look like? Abigail's servant says this to her: "Think it over and see what you can do." What a guiding light those simple words are.

Are you a peacemaker who willingly, unflinchingly walks between opposing forces? Has God ever called you to be such a peacemaker? If your answer is yes, then He has a promise for you:

Blessed are the peacemakers, for they will be called children of God (Matthew 5:9 NIV).

As He was with Abigail, so He is with you, as you do His will!'

The right words in a crisis

What do we do when we are at our wits' end? Abigail's response to this tense situation really struck me. Each crisis is an opportunity. We have differing personalities and emotional bents. Everyone faces storms and tempests. It is crucial for us to know exactly how to respond to hard times. How do we react to crisis? How do we respond to a black day?

Consider Psalm 107:23-32. What do you do when the tempest blows and the waves are lifted high? What do you do when your courage melts away and you reach your wits' end? This Psalmist tells us how to respond. As Christians, we should strive to be calm, cool, and collected. We can accomplish this as we keep a tight rein on our tempers and tongues and allow the Holy Spirit to guide us. Someone said that '"Think twice before speaking once" is wise advice'. William Penn put it this way: 'If you think twice before speaking once, you will speak twice the better for it.' Abigail's example points to the importance of choosing the right words in tense situations. Harsh, loud words may become the catalyst to an unnecessary explosion. They may drive individuals to actions which will be regretted later. In contrast, we see how Abigail's calm, calculated words led to a peaceful solution. This lesson's golden text deserves careful attention:

A soft answer turns away wrath, but grievous words stir up anger (Proverbs 15:1 AMPC).

A word fitly spoken is like apples of gold in settings of silver (Proverbs 25:11 NKJV).

God may permit these hard times to drive us closer to Himself and strengthen our character.

Abigail feared the Lord

Abigail feared God more than she feared Nabal, David, or his merry men. She operated in God's love and because of it she felt bold enough to approach David.

> The fear of man brings a snare, but whoever leans on, trusts in, and puts his confidence in the Lord is safe and set on high (Proverbs 29:25 AMPC).

> There is no fear in love [dread does not exist], but full-grown (complete, perfect) love turns fear out of doors and expels every trace of terror! For fear brings with it the thought of punishment, and [so] he who is afraid has not reached the full maturity of love [is not yet grown into love's complete perfection] (1 John 4:18 AMPC).

Abigail represents something bigger than a godly woman making wise and timely choices. She epitomises how we can leverage God's grace to change lives through intercession.

> For, there is one God and one Mediator who can reconcile God and humanity—the man Christ Jesus (1 Timothy 2:5 NLT).

How did Abigail play the role of a mediator? She took the blame for her husband's offensive actions, even though she was innocent, and pleaded for mercy. In a sense, Abigail sacrificed her life for her household by taking a potentially fatal risk to confront David. This is like what Christ did for us. Max Lucado wrote:

> Just as Abigail placed herself between David and Nabal, Jesus placed Himself between God and us. Just as Abigail volunteered to be punished for Nabal's sins, Jesus allowed Heaven to punish Him for yours and mine (1 Timothy 2:5-6).
> Just as Abigail turned away the anger of David, Christ shielded us from the wrath of God. Though healthy, he took our disease upon Himself. Though diseased, we who accept His offer are pro-

nounced healthy. The result? More than just pardoned, we are declared innocent. We enter Heaven not with healed hearts but with His heart. . . .

Christ lived the life we could not live and took the punishment we could not take to offer the hope we cannot resist. His sacrifice begs us to ask this question: If He so loved us, can we not love each other? Having been forgiven, can we not forgive? Having feasted at the table of grace, can we not share a few crumbs? 'My dear friends, if God loved us like this, we certainly ought to love each other' (1 John 4:11).

To love one another is a command we must obey. You and I must show the Nabals in our lives the grace that God has shown us.

Here is another important point to take away. There are many women today who find themselves in difficult positions. They may suffer in marriages to men who are selfish, proud, and overtly sinful. Their marriages may have started with two professing believers; however, the husband is now hostile to Christianity. Or perhaps the wife was converted after marriage, so life with her unbelieving husband is a daily clash of values. That said, there is a serious warning to Christians, especially the younger generation. I have seen God help some people overcome terrible marriages. It must be emphasised that it is far better to wait than to get into an awful marriage. It is better to hear from God and apply His wisdom to make the right choice of a marriage partner. As the saying goes, 'To be forewarned is to be forearmed'. Marriage should not be entered into lightly or unadvisedly, but thoughtfully and reverently. In her day, Abigail may not have had that privilege, but praise God, you do today.

It is unfortunate that even though some Christians enter marriage thoughtfully, carefully seeking God's guidance, and believing that they have it right, they discover that the person they married has changed beyond recognition. If you find yourself in those circumstances, I encourage you to study the story of Abigail in more detail. She might be your perfect role model. You will derive great instruction and encouragement from her.

I echo the advice of Denise Renner: You may not be facing a specific enemy right now, but Abigail's story gives clear insight into the power of humility, honour, respect, carefully chosen words, and how to defeat your enemies and even cause them to agree with you. I pray this encourages you, as it has encouraged me, to know how to respond when you experience rejection or mistreatment from family members, workmates, and others. Let us learn from Abigail and discover her powerful secrets.

I would say that a godly woman's responsibility of guarding her family is not one that can be done by human strength alone. Praise God for biblical role models such as Sarah, Abigail, and the Proverbs 31 woman. May the Lord grant us the grace, mercy, favour, and strength we need to fulfil that role successfully.

I believe God sends us an Abigail anytime the enemy tries to delay, thwart, or destroy our divine destiny. I am encouraging you to keep God's promises at the forefront of your mind. You have dreams and desires. You know that by God's grace, one day, you are going to accomplish your goals. But maybe, like David in this story, you are in one of those wilderness periods where you see nothing positive happening. It is very tempting to think, *what is the use? It will never happen.* I have been believing for five years, ten years, and twenty years. Let me be the voice of Abigail to you today. Stay the course. Keep believing. You may be tired, discouraged, and frustrated, but do not give up on your future! It may be a long time, but stay focused. God knows exactly where you are and what you are going through. Stay on the high road and keep doing what you know to do.

ESSENTIAL POINTS FROM CHAPTER 4

- The first step to becoming a kingdom wife is to surrender to the lordship of Jesus.
- A kingdom wife should earnestly desire to be strong yet amiable, gentle, multi-talented, resourceful, and hardworking. Like the woman in Proverbs 31, these attributes gain her the respect of her husband and children. **Her fear of God sets her apart as a godly woman.**

- Marriage is a blessing, but it should not be viewed as the source of a woman's value or fulfilment. Only God can be that.
- Women are called *sons of God* just as much as men are.
- There are few things in life more attractive than a woman who knows exactly who God has made her to be and can share her gifts unashamedly, enjoying and celebrating who she is.
- A kingdom woman can have a tremendous impact on her husband's success.
- Every crisis is an opportunity. In facing storms and tempests, it is crucial to know and chose the right response.

Declaration

As a kingdom wife, filled and led by the Holy Spirit, I am creative. I do all my work excellently and prudently, making the most of my time. I am a godly and responsible wife. I rise to every challenge in Jesus. I am an obedient and joyful wife, and no rebellion operates in me. I love my darling husband. He is wise and the king and priest of our home. He makes godly decisions. **My husband and I delight in GOD. We meditate on His law, day and night.** Therefore, our marriage and our family are like a tree planted by streams of water, which yields fruit in its season and whose leaf does not wither. We trust the Lord in all things, and He helps us to do good to each other. We treasure faithfulness in our marriage and in our lives. We build our home on God's wisdom. We live together in harmony and unity with each other, that we might glorify God. We have God's kind of love for each other, growing in patience, kindness, honour, service. We never keep a record of wrongs. We joyfully submit to each other out of reverence for Christ and love like Jesus. **By God's grace,** we do nothing out of selfish ambition. We have humble hearts toward each other, not looking to our own interests, but to the interests of each other. No matter what my husband and I face tomorrow, **God's grace sustains us.**

I declare this by faith in Jesus's majestic name!

Further Study and Scripture References

1 Samuel 15:23; Psalm 1:1–3; Proverbs 21:1, 22:29; Ecclesiastes 9:10; John 14:26; 1 Corinthians 6:19, 12:9, 13:4–8; Galatians 5:22–23; Ephesians 4:29, 5:15–16, 21–30; Philippians 2:3–7, 4:13; Colossians 3:13–14; Hebrews 10:23; James 4:8, 5:16; Revelation 1:6.

CHAPTER 5

The Kingdom Woman as an Excellent Parent

> Train up a child in the way he should go [and in keeping with his individual gift or bent], and when he is old he will not depart from it (Proverbs 22:6 AMPC).

It is a great privilege to be a parent and to be called by God to bring up children. This, to me, is one of the most rewarding, albeit challenging, assignments a woman can carry out in life and I am pleased to share my thoughts and experiences with you on how to raise godly children.

The importance of a mother to her child, and a wife to her husband, cannot be overstated. I believe that women/mothers are called to these important family relationships. Each is a unique gift from God. We are called to protect the sacred unity of these relationships. The world and mothers themselves should recognise and appreciate the importance of motherhood. We should acknowledge mothers as essential caregivers and nurturers of the family. It takes a great deal of sacrifice to do this.

Motherhood Is Ministry

I like this excellent excerpt from Jennifer Alden's article published in one of God TV's newsletters titled *The Joy Of Motherhood—'Godly*

Mothers Are The Nation's Greatest Treasure. She (Jennifer) got the excerpt from Thomas Nelson's *Woman's Study Bible*:

> More than a job or responsibility, mothering is ministry. Most assuredly it takes work! It means sacrifice. Children do not come off an assembly line, nor are they the by-product of an imperial biological process; they are to be lovingly nurtured by their mothers. Mothers divide time among their children but multiply their love for all their children. To this, they add the care of the home, often subtracting many extras to do so.
>
> As a mother lets go of her own life for the sake of her child, she is reminded of the depth and height and breath of God's love for her, and in a unique way she experiences the true joy of motherhood. Godly mothers are the nation's greatest treasure, the Lord's best helpers, and the most blessed among women.

The Maternal Gift

Christian mothers need regular encouragement to help them cope with the challenges of their divine assignment. Whether a woman is approaching marriage, starting a family, or extending her hand to the needy, God has instilled this heavenly gift of loving and nurturing others inside each one of us who *mother*. With or without a physical child of your own, you have been ordained with this maternal gift of life! Mothers give life to others in many ways. From our physical bodies, we give life to the babies growing in our wombs. From our hearts and souls, we give love, care, and nurture to those around us.

My Views as a Mother and Grandmother

I became a mother only thirteen months after my wedding. During this transition, it was easy and natural for me as a first-time mother to give my effort and attention to our new-born. It takes time to adjust to additional family responsibilities, but a godly wife remembers that

116

her husband is her priority. His needs still matter. There will be times she may feel as though she has nothing left to give him at the end of a tough and frustrating day, but she can always run to her King and Lord for strength and energy to remain a wife first and a mother second. Consider this Scripture:

> He gives power to the weak and strength to the powerless. Even youths will become weak and tired, and young men will fall in exhaustion. But those who trust in the LORD will find new strength. They will soar high on wings like eagles. They will run and not grow weary. They will walk and not faint (Isaiah 40:29-31 NLT).

God in His mercy blessed us with more children, and by His grace, grandchildren have now started coming in. All our children are now adults, and each one has proven to be a blessing and a continual source of joy. Praise God!

When my role transitioned from being a wife to a wife and a mother, I expected some changes and had prepared myself for them. However, every stage was different, and things were not exactly as I had imagined them. I took things one day at a time, remaining teachable and trusting God all the way.

When our first child was born, my life changed forever. I found my attention now divided between my husband and our baby. Her arrival introduced new challenges, new logistics to deal with, and additional strains in managing our household, finances, and other concerns. While I expected some of these, reality often surpasses our expectations. But by God's grace, I gradually found ways of making life easier for myself as a new mother, for my husband, and the baby. I had to think about each one of us and build the resilience I needed to cope with the situation. I ensured that my daily routine included such things as taking good care of myself, being practical about problem-solving, and staying connected to my husband deliberately.

The discovery that made the greatest impact on me as a mother and a grandmother was that although motherhood is a great and exciting calling, a gift, and a huge responsibility, it is not necessarily a woman's highest calling. Being a disciple of Christ conferred on me a calling higher than any other. A Christian mother must embrace a role that in its entirety sees bringing pleasure to the Father and glory to Jesus as its ultimate purpose. This role includes being an evangelist and pointing her children and others to the Lord.

The Word of God describes several kinds of callings. Ask Christians what their greatest mission on earth is, and chances are you may get lots of different answers. But there is work that God calls all of us to do, and He laid it out for us in the Bible. It is a mistake to think of our profession or vocation as our greatest lifework, be it as a doctor, caterer, missionary, civil servant, etc. While these are huge, they cannot compare with the highest calling on our lives.

I have seen from personal research and interaction that some Christians believe that marriage is their greatest mission on earth. While agreeing that kingdom marriage is a high calling, from God's perspective, it is not the highest. Others advocate that being a parent is their greatest life assignment. I am blessed to be a mother and can tell you that being a parent is one of the great callings of life. This is so because parenting gives us the wonderful opportunity to discharge the responsibility that God has entrusted to us to shape lives and raise the next generation.

The Scriptures below perfectly summarise the fact that the greatest calling in life, the ultimate purpose of being a Christian, is to **know God and to be conformed in this life to the image of His Son, Jesus Christ.** To replicate Christ in this world, to be temples through whom God lives His life, accomplishes His purposes and reveals His glory. This is a calling that is extended to everyone, to all people.

For we are God's [own] handiwork (His workmanship), recreated in Christ Jesus, [born anew] that we may do those good works which God predestined (planned beforehand) for us [taking paths which He prepared ahead of time], that we should walk in them [living the good life which He prearranged and made ready for us to live (Ephesians 2:10 AMPC).

For those whom He foreknew [of whom He was aware and loved beforehand], He also destined from the beginning [foreordaining

118

them] to be moulded into the image of His Son [and share inwardly His likeness], that He might become the firstborn among many brethren. And those whom He thus foreordained, He also called; and those whom He called, He also justified (acquitted, made righteous, putting them into right standing with Himself). And those whom He justified, He also glorified [raising them to a heavenly dignity and condition or state of being (Romans 8:29–30 AMPC).

And all of us, as with unveiled face, [because we] continued to behold [in the Word of God] as in a mirror the glory of the Lord, are constantly being transfigured into His very own image in ever increasing splendour and from one degree of glory to another; [for this comes] from the Lord [Who is] the Spirit (2 Corinthians 3:18 AMPC).

Let us consider Romans 11:29 from different Bible translations:

For the gifts and the calling of God are irrevocable (NKJV).

For the gifts and the calling of God are irrevocable [for He does not withdraw what He has given, nor does He change His mind about those to whom He gives His grace or to whom He sends His call] (AMP).

God never changes his mind when he gives gifts or when he calls someone (GW).

God's gifts and God's call are under full warranty—never cancelled, never rescinded (MSG).

God never changes his mind about the people he calls and the things he gives them (NCV).

Let us also consider the Scriptures below:

For those whom He foreknew [of whom He was aware and loved beforehand], He also destined from the beginning [foreordaining them] to be molded into the image of His Son [and share inwardly His likeness], that He might become the firstborn among many brethren. And those whom He thus foreordained, He also called; and those whom He called, He also justified (acquitted, made righteous, putting them into right standing with Himself). And those whom He justified, He also glorified [raising them to a heavenly dignity and condition or state of being] (Romans 8:29-30 AMPC).

Since God has called you, you are justified, and if you are justified, He will glorify you, hallelujah!

My sheep listen to my voice; I know them, and they follow me. I give them eternal life, and they will never perish. No one can snatch them away from me, for my Father has given them to me, and he is more powerful than anyone else. No one can snatch them from the Father's hand (John 10:27-29 NLT).

I quote Barnes's commentary on Romans 11:29:

For the gifts—The favors or benefits which God bestows on men. The word χάρισμα charisma properly denotes any benefit which is conferred on another as a mere matter of favor, and not of reward; see Romans 5:15-16; Romans 6:23. Such are all the favors which God bestows on sinners including pardon, peace, joy, sanctification, and eternal life.

And calling of God—The word "calling" κῆλσις klēsis here denotes that act of God by which he extends an invitation to people to come and partake of his favors, whether it be by a personal revelation as to the patriarchs, or by the promises of the gospel, or by the influences of his Spirit. All such invitations or callings imply a pledge that he will bestow the favor, and will not repent, or turn from it. God never draws or invites sinners to himself without being willing to bestow pardon and eternal life. The word "calling" here, therefore, has not respect to external privileges, but to that choosing of a sinner, and influencing him to come to God, which is connected with eternal life.

In fact, in Scripture, the word *call* is used most often to refer to belonging to Christ. This idea or sense of *calling* is especially noticeable in the letters of Apostle Paul.

Including yourselves who are *called* to belong to Jesus Christ (Romans 1:6 ESV).

We are assured and know that [God being a partner in their labor] all things work together and are [fitting into a plan] for good to and for those who love God and are called according to [His] design and purpose (Romans 8:28 AMPC).

The call to belong to Christ is everything. As important as the call to marriage, parenthood, or any kind of work (or ministry) etc. may be, these are all secondary to the call to belong to Christ and to replicate him in the world. Jesus Christ suffered and died for the sins of the world. When we embrace Jesus as Lord and Master, we can make God look glorious in our lives and every other calling including parenthood, work, etc. Our work as Christians must be an integral part of our participation in Christ Himself.

I reiterate that to glorify God with our entire lives is the ultimate purpose for which God created everyone. To insist that motherhood is a woman's highest calling is to imply that all the married or unmarried childless women in the Body of Christ are not living up to the purpose God has for their lives. This is without doubt untrue. It will be a tragic mistake not to see the bigger picture, as we cannot reduce a woman's importance down to whether or not she is bearing and rearing children. **I also reiterate that all women, regardless of whether they are mothers, are of equal importance in the kingdom.**

Regarding parenthood, I believe God wants his married children to be fruitful and multiply; this is a powerful way of extending God's kingdom on earth. The Christian family provides an atmosphere to raise and disciple children in God's ways, so they can disciple their children to impact the world. Every Christian shares the unique call of inviting people that are far from God into the arms of our loving heavenly Father. The family is the primary unit in society, and this is the reason single Christians who desire to marry must pray to marry someone who wants to fulfil God's primary purpose for kingdom marriage—soul winning. Even when single people get married late in life and sometimes cannot have children, they can adopt or foster children or act as spiritual parents and mentors to many children and young adults. The family is a serious part of our calling, God's commission for us to extend His kingdom. He wants us to raise godly, spiritual children. Kevin Paterson with a wonderful insight into this stated:

> There are two ways of making disciples on the earth—first, by reaching the lost and teaching them God's ways; and, second, by reproducing natural children and teaching them God's ways. The latter is often the easier route. Unfortunately, Christians are losing out dramatically to other religions in the world in this "birth-rate evangelism."

Without wishing to cause offence, it is a fact of life that some Christian mothers may not have husbands, while others may have absent husbands who are driven by circumstances to work and live away from home. The father is the pastor of the family, while the mother is the co-pastor. Although the responsibility of nurturing and raising godly children falls on both parents, the father ought to take the lead. As the co-pastor and helpmeet, the mother should always be ready to step up and fill the gap when the father is not there. However, she must be careful not to fall into the trap, by default or otherwise, of setting herself up as the sole driver of the spiritual atmosphere in the home. This is unhelpful and may be dangerous, as the mother may usurp the position conferred on fathers by God Himself.

A common problem in many Christian homes today is where fathers are apparently walking with the Lord but are not providing spiritual leadership for the family. While some Christian fathers have become passive in their families today, many others want to provide spiritual leadership, but just do not know how.

One reason God blessed Abraham was that God knew he would teach his children and raise them in a godly way. This requires insisting that children do what is right. Not just making suggestions and allowing kids to choose what they think is best, as the secular world would want us to do.

> For I have known him, so that he may command his children and his household after him, that they keep the way of the Lord, to do righteousness and justice, that the Lord may bring to Abraham what He has spoken to him (Genesis 18:19 KJV).

This phenomenon handles much of the moral decline in the younger generations, often not knowing for certain what is right and what is wrong. We must not allow ourselves to be pressed into the mould of the world or conformed to it (Romans 12:2).

This should not exclude active involvement of mothers, because Proverbs 1:8 instructs both parents to be equally involved in child upbringing.

> My child, listen when your father corrects you. Don't neglect your mother's instruction (NLT).

Besides, other family members are also encouraged to be role models to their children. An African proverb says, *It takes an entire village to bring up a child*. Paul was reflecting on the generational grace that flowed to Timothy,

> . . . when I call to remembrance the genuine faith that is in you, which dwelt first in your grandmother Lois and your mother Eunice, and I am persuaded is in you also (2 Timothy 1:5 NKJV).

Raising Godly Generations

Kingdom parenting involves intentionally overseeing the generational transfer of the faith in such a way that children learn to consistently live all of their lives under God's divine authority.
—Tony Evans

I sometimes refer to children as awesome wonders. It was a huge blessing and very gratifying for my husband and me when our children made the choice to serve the Lord. When parents question me about what time is best to introduce children to God, I smile and tell them they need to start from conception. The Bible, medical science, and psychology clarify that babies in the womb respond to words and sounds. Luke 1:41 tells us that Elizabeth's baby leapt at Mary's greeting. Since an unborn baby's hearing is developing all the time, he/she can hear after twenty-three weeks. The baby can hear Mum's heartbeat and outside sounds. If both parents have been talking to him or her regularly, the baby can even recognise their voices.

If you are expecting a baby, tell your baby what wonderful plans God has for him/her (Jeremiah 29:11). Tell him/her that by God's grace, you have grand plans to be the most amazing parents. Talk about your dreams and share your life plans with your unborn child. You will never find a more patient or attentive listener. It may surprise you to see that your baby kicks enthusiastically after hearing your voices.

We as parents can do a lot to create an atmosphere where the Lord is honoured. Is it not interesting to note that most people will take several driving lessons to pass a test and get a driving license, but we become parents without a single lesson on parenthood? This is perhaps one reason there are so many disasters in many families.

As a parent today, you may feel that parenting is not as simple as it used to be. Kingdom parenting in a godless society is a challenging task, and I am sure many parents realise that this fight is real. Having and raising children is the expectation in most cultures. You start by falling in love, then you get married, and then children follow.

In the olden days, perhaps husbands and wives did not always devote a lot of conscious thought to the challenge of becoming effective and godly parents. They just did what came naturally. That may have been good enough then, but not in today's technological, fast-paced, and morally mixed-up society.

You do not need to look far to observe the innumerable forces, visible and invisible, that compete for the attention of parents and children alike now. It is not surprising therefore to hear some in the next generation openly announce that they would not want to be parents with the responsibility of raising children in today's world. You wonder, *what has gone wrong?* Could it be that children are misinformed by their parents? Are they exposed to more difficulties because of our modern way of living? This drastic transformation is a wake-up call for Christian parents to find a strategy to raise godly children who look forward to becoming parents at the right time and raising godly children of their own.

One reason God brings two Christians together in marriage is to raise godly children, children who will look like Jesus.

> And did not God make [you and your wife] one [flesh]? And why [did God make you two] one? Because He sought a godly offspring [from your union]. Therefore, take heed to yourselves, and let no one deal treacherously and be faithless to the wife of his youth (Malachi 2:15 AMPC).

Therefore, as a Christian parent, you need to fully understand the primary purpose of having children and why God has blessed and entrusted you with this awesome job. I love Dr. Tony Evans's answer to his own question, 'What was meant by God's instructions to Adam and Eve on day six of the creation account to "be fruitful and multiply, and fill the earth"?' His reply paraphrased was that God intended to reproduce Himself through the process of childbearing and, by the imprint of godly parenting, ensure that God would be replicated all over the world. **In reality, how many Christian parents think of their responsibilities in those terms?**

> So God created man in His own image, in the image and likeness of God He created him; male and female He created them. And God blessed them and said to them, Be fruitful, multiply, and fill the earth, and subdue it [using all its vast resources in the service of God and man]; and have dominion over the fish of the sea, the birds of the air, and over every living creature that moves upon the earth (Genesis 1:27-28 AMPC).

Family Is Very Important to God

Family is the foundation and basic building block of both the church and society. In the very beginning, in the Garden of Eden, God instituted marriage, blessed it, and encouraged the bearing of children. When God blessed Adam and Eve, they had not sinned. I believe God's image would have been automatically replicated in their children if they had children before they disobeyed God. Unfortunately, the divine likeness or image in man was shattered because of their disobedience. Therefore, when a Christian couple has children, only something of the spiritual image of God is replicated in the children.

It is only through the redemptive work of Christ, that our nature is transformed into the full image of God again.

> Who being the brightness of His glory and the express image of His person, and upholding all things by the word of His power, when He had by Himself purged our sins, sat down at the right hand of the Majesty on high (Hebrews 1:3 NKJV).

Therefore, God instructs Christian parents to train their children in His ways:

> Train up a child in the way he should go [and in keeping with his individual gift or bent], and when he is old he will not depart from it (Proverbs 22:6 AMPC).

Child-rearing is a monumental challenge, but also a great privilege. We should teach children who God is, man's condition as a sinner, and our need for a Saviour. It is the responsibility of Christian parents to train and send their children out into the world as express images of the God who created them. This can only be done through diligent obedience to the teaching of God's Word (Deuteronomy 6:6-9) and the intentional guidance in the nurture and admonition of the Lord (Ephesians 6:1-4).

It is our parental responsibility to nurture and shape and sharpen these precious gifts God has given us. **Raising our children to fulfil**

God's plans and purposes for their lives is a serious assignment God has entrusted to every Christian parent. We must raise the next generation to serve their own generation.

Our first parents (Adam and Eve), in the very beginning of creation, represented humanity, and the choices they made would impact every generation after them. I believe God originally intended for their parenting to oversee the generational transfer of faith such that generations after them would learn to consistently live under God's divine authority. Their children would follow their exemplary lives. Unfortunately, Adam committed high treason, and that changed all human history. Notice that in the first generation after Adam, his first son Cain killed his brother Abel.

Thank God for His plan of salvation. God tells us in Deuteronomy 6:2 not only how to raise godly children but also godly grandchildren. **Therefore, our goal and prayer as kingdom parents should be that our godly children raise godly children who raise godly children.**

How Should Christian Parents Raise Godly Generations?

Moses preached the whole of Deuteronomy 6 to the children of Israel as they prepared to enter Canaan. He knew that they were going to face many temptations and enemies in the land they were heading to. Consider his instructions:

> Now this is the commandment—the statutes and the rules—that the Lord your God commanded me to teach you, that you may do them in the land to which you are going over, to possess it, that you may fear the Lord your God, you and your son and your son's son, by keeping all his statutes and his commandments, which I command you, all the days of your life, and that your days may be long. Hear therefore, O Israel, and be careful to do them, that it may go well with you, and that you may multiply greatly, as the Lord, the God of your fathers, has promised you, in a land flowing with milk and honey. 'Hear, O Israel: The Lord our God, the Lord is one. You shall love the Lord your God with all your heart and with all your

soul and with all your might. And these words that I command you
today shall be on your heart' (Deuteronomy 6:1–6 ESV).

Moses's sermon could be summarised as follows: **To raise godly
children or generations, love God passionately, teach your children
diligently, and live in the world circumspectly.** By doing so, God
would bless them, and it would go well with them (Deuteronomy 6:3).
This applies to both single-parent and two-parent families.

I believe that God is a generational God, so He is deeply passionate
about Christian parents raising the next generation. We must see raising our children as a command and a profoundly serious assignment
from God. The Bible is replete with stories of how every generation
lives and impacts the generation after them. For example, Noah's right
standing with God saved his family from the flood. Having lost faith
in humanity in general, God picked out a righteous family, Noah, and
wiped out the rest of the human race in a flood, sparing the animals in
Noah's Ark (Genesis 6:5 and following). On the flip-side, Eli's failure to
discipline his sons (Hophni and Phinehas), who were desecrating the
Holy Place, ended Eli's line of the priesthood. Saul's disobedience cut
off his family from the throne. King David's heart was steadfast after
God in love and worship, resulting in the blessing of his bloodline.

Reading and studying the Bible with a generational mindset will
enable you to appreciate that God is a generational God. Consider how
the impact of parental choices is perfectly displayed where Moses said:

Now listen! Today I am giving you a choice between life and death,
between prosperity and disaster. For I command you this day to
love the Lord your God and to keep his commands, decrees, and
regulations by walking in his ways. If you do this, you will live and
multiply, and the Lord your God will bless you and the land you
are about to enter and occupy.

But if your heart turns away and you refuse to listen, and if
you are drawn away to serve and worship other gods, then I warn
you now that you will certainly be destroyed. You will not live a
long, good life in the land you are crossing the Jordan to occupy.

Today I have given you the choice between life and death,

between blessings and curses. Now I call on heaven and earth to witness the choice you make. Oh, that you would choose life, so that you and your descendants might live! You can make this choice by loving the Lord your God, obeying him, and committing yourself firmly to him. This is the key to your life. And if you love and obey the Lord, you will live long in the land the Lord swore to give your ancestors Abraham, Isaac, and Jacob (Deuteronomy 30:15–20 NLT).

We understand that the choices we make daily affect generations after us. Of course, each generation has its own choices to make, and everyone can become delivered and restored based on their choice to follow the Lord. There is a generational blessing available for our children today if Christian parents will only take their assignment of raising the next generation seriously. Many people today are enjoying the fruits of choices previous generations have made. We must remember that our children will also grow up in the world we leave them.

We have the mandate and responsibility as Christian parents to leave them a better place than we inherited. **Let us, therefore, try by the help of the Holy Spirit to engage in kingdom parenting, intentionally overseeing the generational transfer of our faith so that our children learn to consistently live all of their lives under God's divine authority**.

In my experience, training children involves first leading by example, backed up by reiteration, reinforcement, and encouragement, often many times over. But it is worth it! Children need to be trained mostly in character and the things of God. Some say (and I believe it) that until approximately age eight (that, of course, will vary with the child), the training of children comprises mostly of **input** from their parents. Thereafter, children can begin increasingly to make sound moral judgments from that input they have received.

To raise godly children, be a role model of God's image

Parents are powerful role models for children. They are the first, closest, and ever-constant template their children adopt. So, they must actively display godliness in their own lives for their children to see and emulate. Consider the following Scriptures:

Imitate me, just as I also imitate Christ (1 Corinthians 11:1 NKJV).

Brethren, together follow my example and observe those who live after the pattern we have set for you (Philippians 3:17 AMPC).

The most important requirement for raising godly children is for parents to have a personal relationship with God. We teach our children by the way we conduct ourselves. We well know it that children mimic the behaviour of their parents. Children reproduce the personality and character of their parents. We can never make our children what we are not. We cannot pass on to our children what we do not possess. And we cannot train our children to be godly if we are ungodly. We cannot lead our children to God if we ourselves do not know God.

The good news is that anyone can invite Jesus into their hearts and, by submitting to His discipleship, live a godly life. Parents must, therefore, love God passionately and walk with Him as Enoch did (See Genesis 5:21–24).

Remember, children are quick to detect hypocrisy! For example, before scolding your teenager for excessive screen time, take stock of your own. Of course, it is crucial to set boundaries around technology for children, but it is just as important to **lead by example.** Put your phone away, turn the television off, pick up a book, or go for a walk. Do not just set boundaries for your children, set them for yourself as well.

If you are often irritated and scream at your children at home, but then put on your *Christian* face when you go to church, your children may conclude that Christianity is fake and reject it. If they see parents screaming at each other angrily, not resolving conflicts in a godly way, and then position themselves as an exemplary Christian couple in public, children may decide that Christianity is just a religious game irrelevant to real life. Worse still, if you do not show the fruit of the Spirit (Galatians 5:22–23), then lay legalistic rules on your children to make them look like *good Christians* to others, your children may eventually rebel against you and the Lord.

This does not imply that you must be perfect. What matters is that when you get it wrong, you own up to your faults, apologise, ask for forgiveness, and make necessary changes. That shows what a genuine walk with God looks like, and that you are seeking to be more conformed to the image of Christ. Therefore, if you want to teach your children to follow God, you must love God fervently and have His word in your heart and in your mouth. Be on fire for the Lord and shun lukewarmness like the plague! If your children see you walking with God daily, loving His Word, applying it to your life, and growing in the fruit of the Spirit, your love for God will have a positive effect on them. That is the foundation for raising godly generations. Read God's command to us in Deuteronomy 6:1–6 and Matthew 22:37. Christian parents are reminded that failure to model God in their lives could cause their children to struggle, embrace ungodly examples, and fall away from God.

To raise godly generations, train your children in God's Word

The Bible commands parents to teach their children God's ways of living life. Proverbs 22:6 is a direct promise from God. I always encourage parents to treasure this promise, apply it, and hold on to it tenaciously. It will work for whoever puts it to work. Consider:

> But watch out! Be careful never to forget what you have seen. Do not let these memories escape from your mind as long as you live! And be sure to pass them on to your children and grandchildren. Never forget the day when you stood before the Lord your God at Mount Sinai, where he told me, summon the people before me, and I will personally instruct them. Then they will learn to fear me as long as they live, *and they will teach their children to fear me also* (Deuteronomy 4:9–10. NLT).

And you must love the Lord your God with all your heart, all your soul, and all your strength. And you must commit yourselves wholeheartedly to these commands that I am giving you today. Repeat them again and again to your children. Talk about them when you are at home and when you are on the road, when you are going to bed and when you are getting up. Tie them to your hands and wear them on your forehead as reminders. Write them on the doorposts of your house and your gates (Deuteronomy 6:5-9 NLT).

Teach them to your children. Talk about them when you are at home and when you are on the road, when you are going to bed and when you are getting up (Deuteronomy 11:19 NLT).

For you to raise godly children, you must teach them the Word of God. When our children were young, besides introducing them to God and helping them find God for themselves, we taught them how to read and study the Word of God for themselves. We also taught them how to stand on God's promises and trust Him to meet their needs. I recall how our youngest child could recite chapters of the Bible at seven. I will never forget what she did on one occasion when she took ill at seven. She zeroed in on Isaiah 53:5 and confessed that verse of Scripture over and over and would not stop until healing manifested.

I reiterate the need for Christian couples to study the Word of God together with their children. When our children were growing up, my husband and I read the Bible and prayed with them before the start of the day. As a habit, even now that we are empty nesters by God's grace, my husband and I still read/study the Bible and pray together most mornings and before bedtime.

Paul taught his protégée, Timothy, the importance of training children in the Scriptures from an early age. Everyone in a Christian family should be involved in modelling truth and love to children around. Young adults and mature single people in the church should be included as well. Everyone has a role to play. That Christian parents attend church regularly is not a substitute for helping their children develop a taste for the presence of God for themselves. By bringing them to church, they are encouraged to fellowship with other Christians. Encouragement and the positive challenge from peers play a crucial role especially in teenagers' engagement with the church and the kingdom of God.

Let us consider how the following statistics (in Daniel Whitworth's article of Lakeview church of Christ, Hendersonville, Tennessee, USA, titled: *Will Your Children Go to Heaven?*) were demonstrated in a large congregation in North America. He wrote:

> One congregation found that where both parents were faithful to the Lord, and that includes active interest in the local congregation's programs, 93% of the kids remained faithful. On the other hand, if only one of the parents were faithful, that figure dropped to 73%. Where the parents were only what we call reasonably active in the Lord's work, only 53% of the young people maintained their faith.
>
> Now here comes the shocker: in those cases where both parents attended only infrequently, the percentage of their children who remained faithful to the Lord dropped to 6%.

This underlines the importance of parents being *fully committed* to the Lord and their local church. One purpose of the church is to provide an empowering and supporting environment. Also, to assist parents in bringing up children who know Jesus Christ as their Lord and personal Saviour, who can be people who confidently go into the society as image-bearers of the living God to extend His kingdom in the world. It is not surprising, therefore, that it takes a godly generation to bring up another godly generation.

In Daniel Whitworth's words:

> Want your children to go to heaven? Make sure you are leading them by your faithful example!
>
> Preacher's point—While being faithful does not guarantee the same with your children, it definitely starts them in the right direction. Before the Lord told the Israelites to teach His words to their children, He told them that they must love Him with all their

heart, soul, and strength and have His word in their own heart (Deut 6:5-7). As the saying goes, we must practice what we preach.

If we want our children to go to Heaven, then we must make sure we are headed there ourselves.

Besides cultivating and modelling lifelong habits of loving God, Christian parents must be able to show that God's Word is central in all they say and do. Notice the sequence of command by Moses in Deuteronomy 6:6-9:

Commit yourselves wholeheartedly to these commands
Repeat them again and again to your children
Talk about them when you are at home and when you are on the road, when you are going to bed and when you are getting up
Tie them to your hands and wear them on your forehead as reminders
Write them on the doorposts of your house and your gates (NLT).

Christian parents must abide by God's commands first before they can teach them to their children. When God's Word is fundamental in families and communities, we get closer to raising a godly and discerning generation.

To raise godly generations, parents must pray with their children daily

Hear Apostle Paul's opinion and encouragement:

Always be joyful. Never stop praying (1 Thessalonians 5:16-17 NLT).

Prayer should be your steering wheel and not your spare tyre. We must be spiritually smart enough to put God in the driver's seat of our lives first thing every morning because anything under His control can never be out of control. As late Bob Gass put it:

God can be thought of as our spiritual *Air Traffic Control Tower*. In the actual world, air traffic controllers *see the big picture* with what is going on in the sky. They have the knowledge and authority to instruct pilots to slow down or speed up, fly higher or lower, avoid or navigate through storms, or take alternative routes.

An excerpt from Jennifer Newton's report for Mailonline published in the UK on 4 March 2020 reads:

A record number of flights were handled by UK air traffic controllers in 2019, it has been revealed.

Nats, the UK's provider of air traffic control services, said it managed 2,580,214 flights in UK airspace last year—an increase of 0.9 per cent from 2018.

The last decade also proved to be record-breaking, with Nats saying air traffic increased by 13.3 per cent between 2009 and 2019.

The air traffic control service added that last summer saw its busiest day on record, with its staff handling 8,863 flights on July 5, 2019, beating the previous record set in May 2018.

Meanwhile, it also said that the two millionth flight of year it handled occurred on September 25, 2019—three days earlier than ever before.

With so many flights taking off and landing every minute, pilots must stay in touch with the control tower and take and obey instructions from them to avoid accidents.

Similarly, you must stay in touch with God, who is our all-knowing and all-seeing Control Tower. He is the One who sees the big picture of your life and orchestrates everything that involves you. God makes sure everything that needs to happen in your lifetime happens at the right time and moves at the appropriate speed so you arrive safely at the destination He has for you. Therefore, teaching your children to stay in communication with God should be at the top of your daily to-do list. He will help you and your family navigate the difficulties of life and find your way through cloudy days when you cannot see the next step you need to take.

God wants to be your steering wheel, not just the emergency brake.

It is extremely easy to fall into the trap of using prayer as a crutch only when you are in crisis, instead of making it a part of your day every day. For the married woman, praying together with your spouse and children is not optional. It is a requirement that will cause your family to live in harmony as you worship and seek the face of God together. It is said that a family that prays together stays together.

Kingdom Parents Must Contemplate Their Spiritual Legacy

Leaving a godly legacy ought to be one of our major goals in life as kingdom people. **It has been clearly demonstrated that Christian homes where children are raised according to God's prescriptions will always make a difference in society.** How we live will influence our descendants. I recently researched well-known narratives of two families. Although truth and myth may overlap concerning the historical facts, the point and value remain intact. Let me share these two stories that show the powerful legacy (both good and bad) that parents—especially fathers—create.

The following study by Albert Edward Winship (a pioneering American educator, educational journalist, and a pastor) is typical of the contrast between a godly family (Edwards) and an ungodly family (Jukes) over many generations. Other sociologists told this same story in their own ways. Jonathan Edwards was an American revivalist preacher and philosopher. He was the greatest theologian and philosopher of British American Puritanism, stimulator of the religious revival known as the Great Awakening, and one forerunner of the age of the Protestant missionary. He and his wife, Sarah Edwards, had eleven children. Their descendants were outstanding for their contributions to society. Personal research shows that statistics vary slightly. In 1900, Albert Edward Winship tracked the descendants of Jonathan Edwards. Based on the facts gathered by him, the godly Edwards clan had among their descendants at the time of his study:

- One U.S. vice president
- Three senators, three governors

- Three mayors
- Thirteen college presidents
- Thirty judges
- Sixty-five professors
- Eighty public officeholders
- One hundred lawyers
- Sixty-two physicians
- Seventy-five army or navy officers
- One hundred clergymen, missionaries, and theological professors
- 285 college graduates

There were practically no lawbreakers. Edwards's descendants wrote 135 books and edited eighteen journals and periodicals. Many major industries in America had as their founders or promoter an offspring of Jonathan and Sarah Edwards. Winship lists kinds of institutions, industries, and businesses that have been owned or directed by Edwards's descendants. There is scarcely a great American industry that has not had one of this family among its chief promoters.

What a family!

There was another man who lived in New York at about the same period as the Edwards, known as Max Jukes. The Jukes family was originally studied by sociologist Richard L. Dugdale and described in a book he published in 1877. Max Jukes's legacy came to people's attention when the family trees of forty-two different men in the New York prison system were traced back to him. The Jukes descendants included:

- Seven murderers
- Sixty thieves
- 128 prostitutes
- 140 other convicts
- 280 indigents
- 440 who were physically wrecked by alcoholism

Out of the 1,200 descendants studied, three hundred died prematurely and sixty-seven were reported to have contracted syphilis.

They estimated that Jukes's descendants cost the state approximately $1,308,000. In Dr. Ryan Fraser's article titled *What Legacy Are You Leaving for Your Family?* he stated:

> According to the March 8, 1902, issue of *The School Journal*, the almost universal traits of the Jukes were idleness, ignorance and vulgarity. These characteristics led to disease and disgrace, to pauperism and crime.

What a contrast!

How may this be explained? Edwards was very well known as a godly, hardworking, intelligent, and honourable man. Winship states, 'Much of the capacity and talent, intensity and character of the more than 1,400 of Edwards' family is attributed to Mrs. Edwards'.

It is challenging trying to interpret some confusing information in circulation to untangle fact from fiction, but the contrast between the two family lines cannot be missed, nor the lesson dismissed. It is like darkness and light. What a powerful example of how godly parental example and leadership can wield a powerful influence on children and the generations that follow.

Of course, this does not mean that people are simply a product of their parenting, that who they are is determined entirely by their ancestry. I could not agree more with Dr. Ryan Fraser who said:

> Granted, people aren't merely products of their parenting, good or bad. And, yes, as free moral agents, we can overcome our environments by God's grace and personal resolve. But these are the exceptions, and not the rule. Usually, the apple usually doesn't fall too far from the tree!

The contrasting legacies of the Edwards and the Jukes provide an example of what some sociologists call **the five-generation rule:** How a parent raises their child—the love they give, the values they teach, the emotional environment they offer, the education they provide—influences not only their children but the four generations to follow, either for good or evil. Mark Merrill stated:

What fathers do in their time will reach through the next five generations. The example of Jonathan Edwards shows just how rich that legacy can be. But the five-generation rule works both ways. If we fail to work at being good and godly parents, our neglect can plague the generations that follow.

What a challenging thought! If sociologists studied your descendants four generations after yours, what would you want them to discover? An Edwards legacy or a Jukes legacy? The life you live will determine the legacy you leave.

In no area was Edwards's resolve stronger than in his role as a father. As previously mentioned, Jonathan and his wife Sarah had eleven children. Despite Jonathan Edwards's rigorous work schedule—which included rising as early as 4:30 a.m. to read and write in his library, extensive travels, and endless administrative meetings—he always made time for his children. He committed to spending at least one hour a day with them. And when he missed a day because he was traveling, he diligently made up the hour when he returned. Many books have been written about Edwards's life, work, and influence on American history and his powerful professional legacy. But the legacy that Edwards would probably be most proud of is his legacy as a father.

Consider these sobering words by Mike Merrill:

> The stories of Jonathan Edwards and Max Jukes offer powerful lessons about the legacy we will leave as fathers. Five generations from now, it is likely that our professional accomplishments will be forgotten. In fact, our descendants may know little about us or our lives. But the way we parent today will directly affect not only our children but also our grandchildren, our great-grandchildren and the generations that follow. Dads, we will leave a legacy. What will yours be?

We may not be guaranteed to leave such an impressive legacy as the Edwards. **But by the grace of God, we can make an impact for Christ in this world if we raise godly generations.**

To raise godly generations, parents must discipline children God's way

The Bible teaches Christian parents to discipline their children as part of raising them God's way. The word discipline is from the Latin word *disciplina,* meaning 'instruction and training'. It is derived from the root word *discere,* 'to learn'. The Collins English Dictionary defines discipline as 'the practice of making people obey rules or standards of behaviour and punishing them when they do not'. The word *discipline* tends to have a negative connotation, but it should not. The goal of godly discipline is to set boundaries and create a consistent system of rewarding right behaviour and correcting wrong behaviour.

Couples struggle with disciplining children in many cultures. Secular psychology insists that children are basically 'good'. This is a false assumption that will never lead to biblical discipline. The Bible says:

For everyone has sinned; we all fall short of God's glorious standard (Romans 3:23 NLT).

As previously stated, the divine likeness or image in man was shattered with the fall of man. Therefore, children born to a Christian couple do not have at their birth the full, true image of God. It is only through Christ, the perfect sacrifice of Himself, and our personal acceptance of this sacrifice that anyone can be restored into the full image of God (2 Corinthians 3:18; Acts 4:12).

In recent years, corporal punishment of children has generated heated social and political debate. Many people, including Christians, fail to realise that biblical discipline includes physical punishment—and God tells parents to use it. Sadly, studies show some parents have abused this method of disciplining children. Wikipedia defines *corporal punishment* by a parent or legal guardian as follows:

Any act causing deliberate physical pain or discomfort to a minor child in response to some undesired behavior. It typically takes the form of spanking or slapping the child with an open hand or striking with an implement such as a belt, slipper, cane, hairbrush or paddle, hanger, and can also include shaking, pinching, forced ingestion of substances, or forcing children to stay in uncomfortable positions.

Severe forms of corporal punishment have been reported to include kicking, biting, scalding, and burning. All these make up unlawful child abuse. **This so-called corporal punishment is horrific and bears no resemblance to what the Bible calls discipline**.

Research shows that spanking and other physical punishments, while supposedly for child discipline, are inconsistently applied and often used when parents are angry or stressed. Unsurprisingly therefore, in recent years, some countries removed legal defenses for adult guardians' use of corporal punishment, followed by outright bans on the practice. However, domestic corporal punishment of children remains legal in most countries. Biblical physical punishment is not abuse. That said, there is more to godly discipline than physical punishment.

Remember that the most common discipline that God applies to us is His Word of correction. As parents, we should emulate this. Notice that even with pets such as dogs, a firm word of rebuke often elicits a bow of submission to the owner. Other aspects of biblical discipline include rewards and deterrents, dos and don'ts, setting firm boundaries, and leadership by example.

The Book of Proverbs highlights biblical discipline as the way to life and wisdom. Here are verses that speak about disciplining our children:

> For their command is a lamp and their instruction a light; their corrective discipline is the way to life (Proverbs 6:23 NLT).

> Whoever spares the rod hates his son, but he who loves him is diligent to discipline him (Proverbs 13:24 ESV).

> Discipline your son while there is hope, and do not desire his death (Proverbs 19:18 NASB).

> Train up a child in the way he should go, and when he is old he will not depart from it (Proverbs 22:6 ESV).

Folly is bound up in the heart of a child, but the rod of discipline drives it far from him (Proverbs 22:15 ESV).

Do not withhold discipline from a child; if you strike him with a rod, he will not die. If you strike him with the rod, you will save his soul from Sheol (Proverbs 23:13–14 ESV).

To discipline a child produces wisdom, but a mother is disgraced by an undisciplined child (Proverbs 29:15 NLT).

Discipline your son, and he will give you rest; he will give delight to your heart (Proverbs 29:17 ESV).

To provide balance, David Chakranarayan and Ken Ham wrote:

As part of the command to exercise biblical discipline, God also instructs parents not to *provoke* their children. In other words, discipline in all its aspects—positive and negative, physical and verbal—should be applied, not abusively, but in a way that encourages the child to become the kind of person God intends (which incidentally is the sort of child both parents and teachers want to see).

Fathers, do not provoke your children to anger by the way you treat them. Rather, bring them up with the discipline and instruction that comes from the Lord (Ephesians 6:4 NLT).

Fathers, **do not provoke your children,** lest they become discouraged (Colossians 3:21 ESV) (emphasis mine).

The motivation for discipline

Love and the best interests of the child must motivate any discipline, whether corporal or otherwise. When we discipline our kids, we teach them wisdom and show them right from wrong. If we discipline biblically and in love, our children will grow to respect us as parents. They will learn to respect external authority, whether teachers, government officials, or employers. Biblical discipline reflects how God, our heavenly Father disciplines His children:

> Furthermore, we have had human fathers who corrected us, and we paid them respect. Shall we not much more readily be in subjection to the Father of spirits and live? For they indeed for a few days chastened us as seemed best to them, but He for our profit, that we may be partakers of His holiness. Now no chastening seems to be joyful for the present, but painful; nevertheless, afterward it yields the peaceable fruit of righteousness to those who have been trained by it (Hebrews 12:9–11 NKJV).

Parents Could Be Provoking Their Children in Different Ways

You may be provoking your children by:

- Raising them with aloofness instead of involvement.
- Exposing them to a higher risk of psychological disorders by being too protective or too permissive.
- Speaking badly/spitefully of your spouse in front of your children.
- Showing favouritism or comparing them with others.
- The anger you exhibit while disciplining your children.
- Shaming them.
- Not making them feel special.
- Setting unachievable goals.
- Refusing to admit your faults.

Raise your children with involvement

Too often, we get too preoccupied with our own agenda and get involved in our children's lives only when there are problems. It is irresponsible to have a relationship with our children that lacks depth, but then come rushing in during crises. As parents, we must pursue and befriend our children.

> The parents I most want to imitate are the ones who deliberately build friendships with their children, who have a vision of their grown children being their friends and Christian brothers or sisters, and who then work deliberately toward those goals. These parents give time and attention to their children while they are young, they raise them with kindness and discipline, and they do this by holding in mind the future relationship they long to have.
> —Tim Challies

Protect your children

Avoid the extremes of permissiveness and protectiveness. Overprotectiveness (sometimes referred to as helicopter parenting), may by default shield children from all forms of adversity. This is more harmful than people realise. Whilst parents need wisdom in protecting their children, they must not become so overprotective as to induce fear and other psychological problems.

Research has shown that safe, controlled amounts of acute stress may be good for everyone, including children. Studies have also shown that overprotective parenting can lead to risk aversion, dependency on parents, higher risk of psychological disorders, lack of powerful coping mechanisms, and chronic anxiety. Physical exertion, confrontations on the playground, competitions with winners and losers, minor bumps and bruises, and even periodically experiencing fear are all inducers of acute stress. While parents should strive to protect their children from chronic stress, depriving them of healthy forms of safe stress may leave them unable to deal with stress as adults.

As Christian parents, we must give our children some freedom to make their own decisions (which may include wrong ones) and to experience certain aspects of life for themselves as they grow older. It is wise to protect children by restricting exposure to certain influences until they are mature enough to handle such. Overly protecting children borders on the fear that God cannot protect them. Fear-based parenting creates an inability to cope with life challenges in adulthood. When this happens, children may disconnect from reality. This is simply because, as Renee Davis noted, 'The human mind can do either of the two things at one time—it can either reflect the reality it perceives, or create a reality of its own, not both'.

Permissive parenting leaves children to regulate their own activities, behaviour, and emotions at a young age. Children raised this way have more difficulty self-regulating. Studies have found that children raised by permissive, disengaged parents have less empathy, leading to worse social skills. As Christian parents, we should ask God to help us find the balance between being over controlling and adopting a hands-off approach as we seek to guide our children on their journey to adulthood.

Speak positively about your spouse

Parents must resist the temptation to speak disparagingly about their spouse (deliberately or inadvertently) in front of children. You should not project your hurt, anger, or pain on your children. When you speak badly about someone your child loves and respects, whether or not what you say is true, the consequence is the same. It breaks the child's hearts and places a burden that may be too heavy for them to bear. Unfortunately, it also damages your own standing and credibility with your children and others.

Any parent guilty of this should be quick to retrace their step and apologise to their spouse in front of the children. Doing this leaves a powerful message of what to do when you get it wrong and shows them how to handle such issues in their own lives. The parents could seek God's help and godly counsel to avoid repeats.

> Do not complain, brethren, against one another, so that you yourselves may not be judged; behold, the Judge is standing right at the door (James 5:9 NASB).

Champion your children's uniqueness

Parents must never give children any reason to accuse them of having favourites or comparing them to siblings or anyone else. They must avoid all comparisons to any other children, whether positive (*you have done even better than your brother*) or negative (*it is not as good as your sister's*). Whether intentional or inadvertent, showing favouritism and drawing comparisons are dangerous and divisive. These create resentment and jealousy in a developing child. Such comparisons can also prevent children from finding and peacefully accepting their own place among their siblings. Even normal children will struggle to build themselves up as mentally, emotionally, and psychologically healthy individuals if they feel that they only exist in relation to their siblings. Worse still, parental comparisons of their children create a spirit of competition or rivalry, which damages sibling relationships. It can provoke feelings of inferiority or superiority. This may even happen with an only child when he/she is compared to a cousin or teammate or neighbour's children.

Parents blessed with more than one child would agree that each child is unique and needs to feel unique. In Mathilde De Robien's interesting article titled *Do Your Kids Accuse You of Playing Favorites?* she wrote:

> Some great advice comes from Bernadette Lemoine, psychologist and psychotherapist, and Diane de Bodman, co-authors of a parenting book published in French called *Finding the words that will make them grow and flourish* (Trouver les mots qui font grandir pour les aider à s'épanouir). . . .
>
> While it's easy and tempting for parents to make comparisons in their desire to show their appreciation for their children's temperaments or talents, it's never a good idea to make comparisons in front of them. It divides the children, foments a feeling of inferiority or superiority in them, and creates rivalries and jealousies.
>
> Not only does Lemoine urge parents not to make comparisons, but she encourages parents to teach their children not to compare themselves to each other. She suggests saying something

like, "In our family, we're all different. We don't have to compare ourselves to each other, and we don't have to compete. Comparing yourselves won't gain you any more love from mom and dad. You have to be who you are, with your own strengths and weaknesses."

The psychologist suggests comparing the family to a rainbow to show that each member is indispensable: "Our family is like a rainbow: it's beautiful! You're all different and each one of you counts just as much. The rainbow is beautiful if all the colors are present in it."

The Lord says:

Because you are precious in my eyes and honoured, and I love you, I give men in return for you, peoples in exchange for your life (Isaiah 43:4 ESV).

I believe the Lord would be delighted if we find uplifting words/ gestures to make each child understand that they are unique, and that we love them just as they are, with their strengths and weaknesses. *A parent who suspects rivalry, competition, or jealousy among their children must take appropriate steps to stop any words or behaviour that fan such.*

Remain calm especially while disciplining your children

Many adults testify that their parents used anger or the threat of getting angry as a means of correction and punishment. Discipline was not delivered with calmness and self-control, but with angry slaps or cutting words. Such anger in a parent may lead to anger in a child. In these situations, a parent's anger is unjustifiable, while the child's anger is justified. Anger could discourage children or detract from their emotional balance. Uncontrolled parental anger could also lead to unfair and excessive punishment. God expects parents to discipline and instruct children with patience and kindness. Disciplining your children must be fair, compassionate, and full of love, so you do not harden their hearts toward you.

God commands Christian parents not to provoke their children to anger. As parents, we must deal with our emotions and never let them control us. A practical hint for parents is to train yourself NOT to discipline your children while you are still angry. Wait for the anger to subside (take a prayer walk or do something else until you regain control of yourself).

Hold your children in high esteem

Humiliating your children is emotional abuse. It causes fear in children and, unfortunately, this fear may not go away when they grow up unless God intervenes. Until dealt with, it could become a barrier to a healthy emotional life. When these children become parents, that fear and negativity may be passed through the generations.

Parents who shame their children lose relational equity and tear down trust and self-esteem. Such behaviour may even destroy a child's motivation to engage in the very behaviours you are trying to encourage. Parents can shame and humiliate their children either privately or publicly, by direct or indirect comments. Some parents believe that embarrassing the offending child will deter them from committing that offence in the future. That is not true, and the trust you once had in your relationship may become a thing of the past and be replaced with anger and resentment for the foreseeable future.

I am reminded of a disturbing article I read on the internet about a dad in Tacoma, Washington who filmed his 13-year-old daughter with her long hair cut off and piled on the surrounding floor. She was being punished for sending a boy a racy photo. These were the dad's words heard in the background of the video, 'Man, you lost all that beautiful hair. Was it worth it?' That video went viral—especially after it was revealed that within days, the girl jumped to her death from a highway overpass. This is NOT our portion as the redeemed of the Lord—hallelujah.

If we as parents can remember that we are not perfect, it will become easier to let our children know that it is okay not to be perfect. What we should desire of them is **excellence**, not perfection. We ought to be our children's biggest admirers, mentoring, inspiring, and cheering them as their biggest and most loyal fans. We must always uplift them and never belittle them. As Christian parents, we must monitor our criticisms and ensure children know they come from a place of love. *May the Lord give us the wisdom to discern when we should offer constructive criticism and how to offer it in a way that builds up.*

Make your children feel special

Nothing we say or do as parents will suffice unless we make sure our children feel validated, loved, and valued. It is sometimes easy for parents to get caught up doing our own thing (spending hours on the phone, Facebook, YouTube, and other social media), that we forget to give our children the place, time, and attention they deserve. We must allow nothing, not even our ministry or jobs, to supersede or even interfere with the intimate connection with those we say we love most—those who need us most. *May the Lord show us how to bond with our children and help us be more conscious of making sure our children feel like our top priority.*

Set achievable goals for your children

Years ago, I resigned from my job as an NHS employed biomedical scientist to freelance for personal and family reasons. I recall one locum job in the UK that stood out for its unreasonable and unattainable targets. Because of prejudice, nothing I did was good enough. I knew that I was good at my job. I had brilliant testimonials from previous bosses and my supervisors when I worked for my PhD and from senior academic staff of the Medical School where I worked part time (teaching medical students and trainee doctors). This experience caused me immense stress. I eventually quit that job in search of a place where I felt I could succeed and feel proud of my accomplishments. And I did, praise God!

Do you know that as parents, we set and oversee goals for our children? We must, therefore, make sure that these goals are attainable yet challenging, but never unreasonable. Otherwise, we risk setting them up for failure and exasperating them to the point of discouragement. Parents must avoid the practice of telling their children they were the best in everything from primary through to secondary school—whether in academics or sports—in the mistaken belief that this will challenge and spur kids to greater achievements. *May the Lord give us wisdom when defining our children's goals and expectations, so we are setting them up for success and not failure both for the present and for the future.*

Show humility by admitting your faults

It is no news that our children are constantly watching us to see whether our private lives match up to our conduct in public. Whether children or adults, they are observing to see whether we model the Christ-like behaviour we expect from them. They are watching to see how we respond to life's challenges and what we do when we mess up.

As Christian parents, it is important to be trustworthy. We must trust God to help us resist the urge to model a deception of perfection. It blesses our children when we make mistakes, if we are willing and able to deal with them openly, with humility and honesty. It encourages them to see us own up to our mistakes, accept responsibility for our actions, apologise, and ask for forgiveness where necessary. Some children in Christian homes are hurting today because parents portray perfection and refuse to admit their faults. If you are guilty of this, ask the Lord to help you to become real and model authenticity to your children.

....

ESSENTIAL POINTS FROM CHAPTER 5

- The greatest calling in life is to know God and to be conformed in this life to the image of His Son, Jesus Christ.
- All women, whether they bear children or not, are of equal importance in the kingdom of God.

- The family is God's plan and vehicle for us to extend His kingdom by raising natural and spiritual children.
- One reason God blessed Abraham was that God knew he would teach his children and raise them in a godly way.
- To raise godly children, Christian parents must apply scriptural injunctions and principles with determination, diligence, and doggedness practically in their everyday interactions with their children.
- Children raised in a godly manner are more likely to raise godly children themselves, fulfilling the five-generation rule.

Declaration

Father, thank you for my family and for the gift of motherhood. What a joy and blessing my husband and children are to me! I declare and decree: Because I believe in the Lord Jesus Christ, I am a kingdom parent. I parent with Christ at the centre of my home. I train my children up in the right way, and even when they are older, they will not depart or be swerved from it. My entire household is sold out to Jesus and blessed beyond measure with every spiritual blessing in Christ. Goodness and mercy follow us. My children shall be mighty on the earth, for the generation of the upright are blessed. They shall be as signs and wonders in the earth. My children will flourish like olive plants around my table. They are a gift from the Lord. My children are like arrows in the hand of a warrior. My sons in their youth are as grown-up plants and my daughters as pillars fashioned as for a palace. The Lord has established our household as His own. He causes us to succeed. The Lord surrounds my family with favour as a shield. No weapon formed against us as a family prospers. What the Lord has blessed, no man can curse. We live under the shadow of the Most High, therefore no evil shall befall us and no disaster comes near us. My children hold fast to God's Word and ways. They treasure God's commandments and they cry for discernment. The spirit of wisdom is poured out upon my children and my children's children, and words of wisdom are being made known to them. The Power of God will consume all our problems. Our expectations shall not be cut off. The name of the Lord shall protect me and my family.

I declare this by faith in Jesus's majestic name!

Further Study and Scripture References

Deuteronomy 6:6-9, 28:1-12; Joshua 24:15; Psalm 5:12, 84:11, 91:1,10, 112:2, 127:3,4, 144:12; Proverbs 1:23; 2:2-3, 22:6; Song of Solomon 2:4; Isaiah 8:18, 59:21, 44:3-5, 54:13,14,17; Matthew 5:6,8, 6:13; Acts 2:17, 16:31; Ephesians 1:3; Jude 2.

CHAPTER 6

The Kingdom Woman As a Marketplace Minister

To be anointed for business is to be set aside by God for service in the marketplace.

Once anointed, we are to use our job as a ministry vehicle to transform the marketplace so that the gospel will be preached to, and heard by, every creature in our sphere of influence
—Ed Silvoso

Discovering and fulfilling your God-given purpose in life is what God calls each of us to do. If you are reading this today, you may be looking for more effective ways to extend God's kingdom in your sphere of influence.

I have been privileged to understand that ministry takes place in our vocation or sphere of influence. Being a kingdom man or woman called to ministry in the secular world is difficult, but that is the challenge that inspires a warrior's spirit to attempt great things for God in the marketplace. I hope this chapter will help you understand that your work is a major part of your calling, therefore, make a difference today in whatever God has called you to do.

Effective Marketplace Ministry

We have a mission in the marketplace—Matthew 5:13–16 and 28:16–20.

The key point here is God's call for Christians to understand that our spiritual life was never meant to be separated from our work and business. They should be the same. It was never God's intention for His people to separate what they do on Sundays from what they do on other days of the week. Bill Winston stated:

> Taking your faith to your workplace and business should look exactly like what you do with your faith when you are in church. The only difference is the location.

God wants His people to be filled with the knowledge of His will, to know how to operate in their sphere of influence. He wants the world to see that something is different about our lives. The Lord wants us to incorporate ministry into our careers and businesses. He is raising up marketplace ministers who understand how our spiritual lives blend with our secular jobs or businesses. In these last days, God is raising up people with a distinct kingdom mindset. He wants us to see the need to identify our playing fields if we are to touch our generation for Christ. Kingdom people in the marketplace must all understand that work and business are vehicles to touch lives. No matter what you do, whether you are a joiner, bus driver, doctor, lawyer, business owner, farmer, administrator, nurse, **you are an ambassador for the kingdom of God in your sphere of influence.**

In God's kingdom, work or business is worship. God has made us kings and priests (Revelation 1:6). In Bill Winston's words:

> In God's Kingdom, you function either as king or as a priest. Kings take care of the more secular business matters of the community. They are marketplace ministers who serve in government, business, education, media, family and arts, and entertainment etc. Priests take care of the more spiritual matters. They are those who serve as apostles, prophets, evangelists, pastors, or teachers, or what is commonly referred to as the five-fold ministry. God is calling for the restoration of the inseparable team of kings and priests to bring faith back into the marketplace, and to accelerate the advancement of His Kingdom around the world in these end times.

It is crucial for Christians in these last days to understand how Ekklesia (as Jesus taught it) is the vehicle for transforming nations and how it applies to our entire lives as His followers. Hear this reflection on Ed Silvoso's book *Ekklesia* after Adam (a marketplace minister and research analyst) completed a Worship Works course applying Silvoso's teaching:

> Jesus demonstrated throughout his earthly ministry that he would constantly challenge mind-sets in order to bring people back to the Father's heart. In his book, 'Ekklesia', Ed Silvoso summarises it like this: 'Tradition must be a propeller, and not an anchor, in order to enable us to successfully transition from the old to the new'.
>
> As I reflect on reading 'Ekklesia', the key theme for me is 'making disciples of all the nations', by adopting a person, a place or an institution in prayer. In order to bring the kingdom of God to the places God has called us to be, we have to be invested in it, to understand and feel the needs of that place. Passivity helps advance nothing.

My all-embracing aim is to prod every believer towards fulfilling their divine calling in whatever place that God has positioned them for such a time as this. He is not going to score you on your performance at work or business success as the world does. Instead, God is looking for fruit and the eternal impact you produce as a Christian marketplace minister. Our vision as marketplace ministers should be to see a transformed marketplace due to its collision with Christ.

What Is Marketplace Ministry?

Wikipedia defines *marketplace ministry* as:

> Evangelism or other Christian activities that are targeted towards the secular workplace, as opposed to homes, churches, or specialized venues. It can also refer to particular parachurch organizations that focus on such ministry.

There are other definitions of marketplace ministry, but I like Chris Patton's: 'A disciple, witness, or an ambassador for Christ in and through their work or business'. A comparable approach is having the attitude of being a full-time minister in the workplace.

Marketplace Ministry Is Not Less Than Pulpit Ministry

Marketplace ministry is not a backup Christian life, but a sacred calling. As a marketplace minister you are supposed to serve God in your business and secular job as an ambassador. **It is an unfortunate mindset if you think your secular job or business is solely for putting bread on the table.** Your marketplace ministry is all about honouring God with what you have and who you are. It is not an add-on to your Christian commitment, but an expression of who you are serving—God.

For many years, Christians involved in business and secular occupations thought their only usefulness to the kingdom comprised of what substance/wealth/finance/experience they bring from their jobs towards the smooth running of the church. They consistently felt inferior to and thought of themselves as second-class citizens compared to full-time missionaries/ministers. I cannot emphasise enough that such a mentality is appalling and nonbiblical. Unfortunately, it is still common among Christians today. God is changing this mindset in these last days. Clinging to this perspective could encourage some to attempt a pulpit or fivefold ministry to which they have not been called. Vocational, fivefold ministry is not for all Christians and should not be assumed without a clear and certain call. Yet many people who have not received the call to pastoral ministry still have a burning desire to serve the Lord.

The good news is that serving God does not always mean becoming a pastor or a missionary. **If you venture outside the call and gift of God, you will not have the grace and anointing to do the job. Worse still, this could be disastrous not only for the one who has wrongly discerned God's call and gone on to the pulpit, but even more unfortunate for those who wind up under such leadership.** You are called to do ministry right where you are! Whether in business, education, home-schooling, medicine, or anywhere else, you can be active in Christian ministry right there! Unless God specifically says otherwise, there is no need to leave the area of your calling (1 Corinthians 7:17, 21). In fact, there is a need right where you are.

The kingdom of God needs ambassadors in every area of society. That can never happen if the apostles, prophets, evangelists, pastors, and teachers are the only ones left to do the work of the ministry. These are the gifts from God to equip the saints for the work of the ministry.

> And He Himself gave some to be apostles, some prophets, some evangelists, and some pastors and teachers, for the equipping of the saints for the work of ministry, for the edifying of the body of Christ (Ephesians 4:11-12 NKJV).

God's plan is for the actual work of the ministry to be done by dustmen, professors, plumbers, landscapers, market traders, lawyers, nurses, etc. Jesus Christ is our best example. He understood the idea of the marketplace completely. Search the Scriptures for yourself and see how He integrated workplaces with His life's mission. The Lord spent little time behind synagogues or temple walls. Most of His time was spent in the marketplace. Let us consider these facts compiled by Os Hillman, the Founder and Executive Director of Marketplace Leaders Ministries:

> The New Testament records that Jesus appeared publicly 132 times—122 were in the marketplace.
>
> Jesus told 52 parables—45 had a workplace context.
>
> Acts recorded 40 divine interventions—39 were in the marketplace.
>
> Jesus spent His adult life as a carpenter until the age of 30 when He began a public preaching ministry in the workplace.
>
> Jesus called 12 workplace individuals—not clergy—to build His church.
>
> Work is *worship*. The Hebrew word *avodah* is the root word for both *work* and *worship*.
>
> Work in its different forms is mentioned more than 800 times in the Bible.

Also consider the patriarchs of the Jewish and Christian faith, Abraham, Isaac, and Jacob. Each one of these men was a phenomenally successful businessman. Dr. Ferdinand Nweke echoes this idea in his book *Marketplace Ministry—Using Your Platform In The Marketplace to Transform Lives, Cities and Nations*. He writes:

[God] is redefining "ministry", "minister", "full time", "a man of God", and other exclusive terms that have sidelined many kingdom laborers. He is raising a new generation of marketplace ministers who will reach the world from their platforms in the marketplace. They will take the church out of [the church building] and carry it to the various corners of the world—to people in businesses, government offices, arts and entertainment, the media, education etc . . . Their minds will be full of heaven but they will be manifestly relevant on earth. Their ministry will bring the light and power trapped in the church into every facet of society.

Ed Silvoso said this in his book *Anointed for Business*:

Unfortunately many of these marketplace Christians feel like second-class citizens when compared to people who serve full-time in a church or missionary context. This should not be the case. No matter the occupations, Christians who work at secular jobs need to know that they are not perpetual privates in God's army just because they have not gone to seminary. They need to discover that they have the potential to become full-fledged generals whose ministry is in the heart of the city, instead of inside a religious building.

It is imperative that they realize that not only is it OK to do ministry in the marketplace, but that God has explicitly called them and anointed them for it. By "anointed" I mean that they have been chosen and empowered by the Holy Spirit for a divinely sanctioned assignment. By "ministry" I mean that they can do more than just witness; they can bring transformation to their jobs and then to their cities—as happened in the first century.

As a kingdom citizen in the marketplace, you are called to establish God's kingdom on Earth. Without your active participation and leadership, our cities will not be transformed, and we will not fulfil the Great Commission in our generation. We are fully qualified and anointed ambassadors of the Empire of Jesus, the High King of the universe. God has entrusted to us the message of reconciliation, the good news that Jesus reconciles sinners to God.

We must always remember that wherever we go, and whatever we do, we are ambassadors for the King. **When we hang out with business partners, neighbours and friends, we are ambassadors for the King. When we go to our places of employment, take part in meetings, work on projects, welcome clients, or even when we are out shopping, we are still ambassadors for the King.**

Here is an excerpt from a powerful article titled *God Wants Everyone in Full Time Ministry?* I found on the Christ For All Nations (CFAN) website. It reads:

Through the years a fundamental disconnect has evolved between two parts of the church commonly known as the clergy and the laity. A hierarchical concept of ministry has evolved, which has segregated the two groups. **This has resulted in a crippled system in which the career ministers, who are a minority of the church, have assumed the majority of the work of the ministry.** Meanwhile the rest of the Body of Christ, the majority, have been taught that they are not qualified for ministry and have been reduced to a crowd of spectators.

But when Ephesians 4 talks about the role of the apostles, prophets, pastors, teachers, and evangelists, the concept that emerges is very different from what has been modelled in the modern church. The New Testament pattern is for those in fivefold ministry offices to serve the Body of Christ by equipping the saints for the work of the ministry (Eph. 4:12). **If the Body of Christ were compared to a football team, those in fivefold ministry would be the water boys, serving the team and helping to keep them equipped and refreshed.**

The real ministers and ambassadors of God's Kingdom

to the world, the real players on the field, are the hundreds of millions of blood-washed saints who make up the body of Christ. What a tragic loss we have incurred by perpetuating the mentality that the few of us in fivefold ministry are the 'real' ministers and the rest are just spectators.

My friend, God wants to use the gifts, talent, and calling that He's given you to impact the world for His glory. Use whatever sphere of influence He places you in to further His Kingdom and authority!

My Stories: Entrepreneur and Career Woman

I worked as a secondary school teacher, research officer, biomedical scientist, and business owner for decades before I heard the term *marketplace ministry*, where you intentionally incorporate ministry into your career or business. Unfortunately, we still have many pastors and church leaders today who do not see these truths, let alone adequately teach them. The closest I ever heard of was the Full Gospel Businessmen's Fellowship International (FGBMFI). In fact, I was a member of the FGBMFI in Benin City, Nigeria, in the late 80s, but nobody knew about or taught marketplace ministry the way we know it today.

As a Christian, I knew that I loved Jesus and that it was mandatory for me in obeying and fulfilling the Great Commission to share my faith wherever I went—including at my job and business.

> Then the eleven disciples went to Galilee, to the mountain where Jesus had told them to go. When they saw him, they worshiped him; but some doubted. Then Jesus came to them and said, 'All authority in heaven and on earth has been given to me. Therefore, go and make disciples of all nations, baptizing them in the name of the Father and of the Son and the Holy Spirit, and teaching them to obey everything I have commanded you. And surely I am with you always, to the very end of the age' (Matthew 28:16–20 NIV).

I was not taught and never met believers who were intentional about bringing their faith to the workplace or business. My functioning as a marketplace minister began in the past seven years when I first heard it taught by Ed Silvoso, the faith-driven entrepreneur, founder and president of Harvest Evangelism, and the leader of the Transform Our World Network. I caught the vision then and ran with it. Today there is a new paradigm, what I call *the marketplace paradigm shift*.

We are in the end times and God is raising marketplace ministers with a kingdom mindset. God wants us to get hold of His priorities in the end times, to bring church to our work and touch people with the power and life of Jesus. Why separate the part of us that loves God from the part that physically operates in the marketplace? Integrated faith and work are made possible because this is precisely what Jesus Christ did. He is our model, and strength.

Putting Your Faith on Display at Work

Jesus said:

> Therefore everyone who confesses Me before men, I will also confess him before My Father in heaven. But whoever denies Me before men, I will also deny him before My Father in heaven (Matthew 10:32–33 ESV).

You must always identify yourself publicly with Jesus. I like the way Greg Gilbert and Sebastian Traeger put it in their blog:

> Learn to put God on the table. . . . When someone asks what you did over the weekend, tell them you went to church. Mention the Bible study you attend on Tuesday nights. Don't just mumble, "I'm sorry I can't come to your birthday party; I'm busy." Say, "I can't come because I'm scheduled to work at my church's clothes closet this weekend." You do not have to be obnoxious or irresponsible about it. Just make sure you identify yourself publicly with Jesus. Let people know somehow you are a Christian and do not mentally censor your Christianity out of your interactions and conversations. You'll be amazed at how often people will take the

opportunity to press in on the little piece of information you've just offered. People are often more interested in spiritual things than you think. They just need a bit of permission from you to feel free to talk about it.

I believe God wants us kingdom people to fellowship with one another and work to mentor others, so that the next generation of people of faith called to the marketplace know that they play a very important role in the kingdom. God positions His people in strategic places to be salt and light in this dark and fallen world and to bring others to His kingdom. God wants to use the gifts, talents, and calling that He has given you to impact the world for His glory. Use whatever sphere of influence He places you in to further His kingdom and authority!

Since I caught the vision of marketplace ministry, I have had the privilege of encountering people in such ways I could never have orchestrated but for God's favour and prompting. In fact, I regret missing so many opportunities to minister to others. Praise God, every day is a chance to listen to the prompting of the Holy Spirit as we work out our kingdom assignments. We are threads in the tapestry that the Lord is weaving to advance His kingdom. I have seen God's kingdom advance through ministry to people in the marketplace in powerful ways.

One of my favourite encounters in the marketplace occurred in Dublin, the capital of the Republic of Ireland. I was the only person of colour in the department. I recall how a colleague of mine, also a contractor biomedical scientist, was fired. I was consulted before the final decision was taken and also left to comfort the distraught gentleman after he got the sad news. He was inconsolable, a sixty-three-year-old man sobbing like a baby. After work on that unforgettable day, I went with him to his hotel room, just to make sure he did not harm himself, and stayed with him until he was reasonably composed. He was due to catch his flight back to the UK the following day. Before work the following morning, I visited again and assured him that his contract termination was not the end of life. God gave me an opportunity to share the gospel with him and he readily accepted Jesus into his heart. Once he embraced Jesus, suddenly, his contract termination did not seem to matter that much. He left a completely transformed and joyous man. That is the power of the GOSPEL. Praise God forevermore!

I also recall what the senior consultant and Head of the Department of Microbiology in the hospital I worked in (in Glasgow, UK) said to me on my last day at work. I resigned from the NHS Trust because my family was moving to the Isle of Man. I went around the department to say farewell to my colleagues and bosses. He said, 'Mrs Nwabineli, we have watched you these years you worked in this department. We realise you are in touch with a Supreme Being. Whoever this is, stay with Him and keep on doing what you have been doing'.

Glory to God! Although no one gave their life to the Lord while I worked there, I am confident that something about God and His kingdom was deposited there for eternal purposes. I believe that what God used me to plant would somehow in God's timing and season eventually yield fruit for the kingdom.

Fear Freezes Faith and Cripples Creativity

Fear permitted and/or tolerated is faith contaminated. In the famous parable of the talents in Matthew 25:14–30, Jesus said the master gave three people talents to invest, each one according to his ability. It is important to realise that God will give you only what you can handle. If you did not get the same talents as your neighbour, do not worry. Just use what you have been given. The first crucial message of this parable is that everyone has something; no one is left with nothing.

In this parable, the first two servants doubled their talents. But the third shows us another perspective to life. There are people who cave in to fear and bury their heads in the sand like the proverbial ostrich. He had his reasons for hiding his treasure, but no reason is ever good enough to make us hide our gifts and talents.

Another vital lesson here is that the one who failed to invest lost it all. What God gives us, He expects us to use and be a blessing with it. When we do not use what we have, we may lose our return and rewards. God does not like to waste His resources.

Your talents are seeds that must be sown. Sow them into something you believe in, something that will outlive you. God wants you to multiply everything you have. Christ's parable ends with some very sobering words, 'Take the talent from him and give it to the one who has the ten talents' The Bible teaches:

Having then gifts differing according to the grace that is given to us, *let us use them* (Romans 12:6 NKJV).

When we are not operating in our areas of giftedness, we struggle. So, we need grace in our gifting, and grace for the areas in which we are not gifted. In my experience, the more I use my gifts and talents, the better I become, and the greater the grace released in opportunities and resources that become available to me. I believe this is true for all of us.

Starting Your Own Business: Businesspeople in the Bible

The Book of Proverbs seems to be a good place to start. The woman described in chapter 31 has such outstanding abilities that she deserves to be studied by everyone. Her family's social position seems to be quite high. She is portrayed as a great wife, mother, and efficient manager of her home. An astute businesswoman who runs her businesses well, she cooks, she sews—what she does not seem to do is get tired. I encourage kingdom women to learn from her industry, integrity, and resourcefulness.

Jesus and His earthly father Joseph were in the carpentry business before Jesus began His ministry (Matthew 13:55; Mark 6:3). The Greek word used here is *techno,* a root expression describing craftsmanship, skill, and art, just as in some modern cultures, those who work with wood do not just do carpentry work but are builders who build houses mainly out of wood. Therefore, Jesus and Joseph may have been craftsmen; artisans skilled in building from wood, not just doing carpentry work.

Apostle Paul was not only an intellectual scholar and lawyer, he was also a skilled tentmaker (Acts 18:1–3). Priscilla and Aquila, his companions during his second missionary journey in Corinth, supported themselves by making tents while serving Christ. They opened their home to Paul, who joined them in tent making.

Lydia was a successful businesswoman, specialising in costly purple cloth. The first convert in Philippi and Europe, she brought her entire household to hear Paul talk about Jesus and all were baptised as a result. She also housed Paul and Silas. Lydia's conversion is found in Acts 16:11–40.

These all combined a love for Jesus with expressing their gifts and abilities at work. Before then, Luke continued his marketplace calling as a doctor while writing the Gospel of St Luke and the Acts of the Apostles. He also accompanied Paul on at least one missionary journey.

> Only Luke is with me. Bring Mark with you when you come, for he will be helpful to me in my ministry (2 Timothy 4:11 NLT).

We are not told that Cornelius resigned from the Roman army after his household accepted Jesus as Lord.

Besides what God has invested in you through talents and abilities, you also understand that you are a gift yourself. This means that you are a primary gift and inside you are gifts that are to be given away. For instance, your gift might be in your ability to speak a word of hope to people grappling with feelings of hopelessness and despair, or showing acts of love and kindness to someone needing your genuine concern, or tenderly taking someone by the hand and giving them your time until you help them find their way. It may be to rescue teenagers or children, or assisting the next generation in knowing the joys of serving Jesus, or reaching out and investing in women to become virtuous women.

Personal Experience

By God's grace, I express some of my creative talents and abilities as a specialist cake artist and trainer in my confectionery business. I bake, design, and decorate cakes for special occasions including weddings, birthdays, and other celebrations. I also train people from different walks of life in cake artistry and sugar-craft. This gives me the incredible opportunity to express my creative, imaginative, innovative, and artistic abilities. It is also a powerful avenue to extend the kingdom of God.

Entrepreneurs must be prepared to face and overcome a host of challenges when starting their own businesses. It can reward at last, but sometimes tough obstacles await as you step out in faith. Here are some hurdles associated with the entrepreneurial process which I faced when I built my business from scratch.

Being the visionary and developing the business idea

It is generally agreed, *find a solution to a problem facing people and you have a potential business in the making.* This applies to the confectionery business I currently run. As the founder, I am expected to come up with ideas. This was the first quandary I faced. Finding the right business opportunity or creatively developing an idea is not a straightforward task. To get started, I had to see what others could not do. While others probably saw problems, I saw opportunities. But it quickly dawned on me that seeing opportunities was just the beginning.

The key business challenge was going to be my ability to forge that opportunity into a business idea. But God used my daughter, Ngozi, and my local council (Gateshead Council) to overcome this challenge. Gateshead Council had a problem—establishing another confectionery business in a trading estate within their area of jurisdiction, called Team Valley. Since I had registered with them as someone looking to establish a business around confectionery, they approached me and asked if I was interested in working with them to solve their problem. My daughter and I wrote a detailed, professional, and convincing business plan which was unanimously approved. In addition, they also provided business premises and paid half the costs of equipping it—praise God! All because I was prepared to step out and take the risk of turning an idea and a passion into a business.

Finding the right business location

Did I want a location that has a rapidly booming population, good road network, and other amenities at a good price? My local government council found me excellent premises in a suitable location. That minimised the challenge.

Financing

This was easy because I had a pool of capital from my secular job and the Council was also prepared to give me a small start-up grant. As the business developed and expanded, I started networking and thinking through other funding options.

Assembling a business team

I am talking about the *strategic round table business team* that will meet regularly to brainstorm on ways to grow a business. Thankfully, Gateshead Council made this possible. They inserted me into a group of professional business advisers who worked for them. I found my business team very vital, as their input helped me raise venture capital successfully. I believe every passionate and serious entrepreneur is bound to have strengths and weaknesses. That is the reason they need a business team to complement their weaknesses.

A team is a necessity for building a successful business. It was my responsibility to transfer my passion and vision to my team of advisors. I made them see the same future that I saw at the start of my business. I had to be passionate and hardworking enough to make them believe in my possibilities and be passionate about making that possibility a reality. Although an ideal strategic business team should include a banker and accountant, these were absent in my team as I had to use the advisory team Gateshead Council provided for budding businesses.

Finding good and loyal apprentices and employees

Finding an apprentice or employee is not simply presenting the job description and waiting for the right candidate to surface. There is much more to it than that. It is tough to find a hardworking and trustworthy employee. Many want to work less and get paid more.

Finding an outstanding employee who will be passionate about their job is arduous. But hiring excellent employees is a minor task compared to forging your employees into a team. You may have exceptional employees, but if they are not interested in the business's growth, and cannot act as a team, they are a risk and will yield nothing but stagnation. A football team may have skilled players, but their individual skills may not win them the matches and prizes they deserve.

Apprentices and employees are the representatives of any business to customers and the outside world. They are supposed to reflect the business culture and ethics. If just one employee is rude to a customer, this portrays a poor image for that company. Bad news travels fast! So, I have been incredibly careful when hiring apprentices and employees. I now also stick to the golden rule of business—hire slow and fire fast.

Finding good and loyal customers

In building my business, I came across good and bad customers. These days I am on guard for the bad ones. Good customers are hard to find. The good customers I have are loyal to my company and will forgive me if I make a mistake and apologise. They try to do the right things that will benefit both themselves and my company. Bad customers will always look for loopholes in the company's policy to make a few gains. They will always try to exploit the company's goodwill and look for ways to rip off the company. Good customers build your business, but bad customers, if they are many, may liquidate your business. Just as I fire bad apprentices and employees, I have also learned to fire bad customers without hesitation. I no longer invest my time and effort in customers that simply are not worth it!

Decision-making

This is probably the most stressful part of this list. As an entrepreneur, I must make several decisions a day, from big, company-impacting decisions, to tiny, hour-affecting ones.

Dealing with competition

Many individuals may see competition as a plague. I see competition as a wonderful challenge and a benchmark for creativity, the primary engine that stimulates innovation and production of quality products at great prices. Without competition, there will be no innovation and without innovation, your business will become stagnant. Therefore, I embrace competition. It keeps me on my toes and drives me to constantly improve my products and services.

Unforeseen business challenges and expenses

Just as a ship's captain or pilot is always on the watch for unpredictable poor weather, thunderstorms, and technical failures, so a good entrepreneur must always be prepared for whatever troubles are lurking. Unexpected problems can come in many forms, and a strategy for mitigating risk should be part of the day-to-day thinking of a businessperson. Difficulties not handled properly can ruin one's plans to build a successful business.

Another issue I faced after my business took off was an unforeseen increase in business expenses and rent for the premises. If this is not handled properly at the start, it may cause negative cash flow and eventually business failure.

*Advertising and creating an awareness
of my presence in the community*

I paid a professional web designer to set up a functional, accessible, and mobile-friendly website (thebestdesignercakes.com). Although expensive, it helped to make my business look very professional and attracted many customers. I also used two of the big local listing services (the Yellow Pages and the Advertiser) to create an awareness of my presence in the community. I embraced social media (Facebook and Instagram) and advertised in local church magazines as well. I built my network on LinkedIn.

The most effective means to date is word of mouth. Satisfied customers who are not affiliated with my company talk about my business and recommend my products to other people. Kind admirers/ well-wishers and satisfied customers advertise my services for me for free. Regular business interactive meetings organised by Gateshead Council were other effective ways of creating awareness of my services in the community.

Never Give Up

You need *purpose* and *persistence* to live your best life. Your determination and refusal to give up are the essence of purpose and determination. When you get started and you fail, try, and try again. Failure is part of every success. History is filled with people who are famous for doing great things, yet their lives were often dotted with miserable failures before they succeeded. Keep persevering and you will win. A person who refuses to give up will eventually succeed. If your dream does not come through immediately, do not get discouraged. Continue to pursue your skills and develop your talent. Keep on studying and learning. Grow by experience and keep working. Victory goes to anyone who is willing to 'fight one more round'. Always remember that when you quit, God can do no more for you. But when you persevere in His might, He will come to your aid.

Here is a Scripture you might want to meditate on and commit to memory:

For the Lord GOD helps Me, Therefore, I am not disgraced; Therefore, I have made My face like flint, And I know that I will not be ashamed (Isaiah 50:7 NASB).

Here are the powerful and inspirational words written on the historic monument commemorating the life of author Jack London, who wrote the classic *White Fang*:

I would rather be ashes than dust! I would rather my spark burn out in a brilliant blaze than that it should be stifled by dry rot. I would rather be a superb meteor, every atom of me in magnificent glow, than a sleepy and permanent planet. The function of a man is to live, not to exist. I shall not waste my days trying to prolong them. I shall use my time.

If you are serious about making a difference in this world, you must discover, enhance your God-given assignment(s) or talent(s), and commit yourself to it/them 100 percent. Paul did that.

But my life is worth nothing to me unless I use it for finishing the work assigned me by the Lord Jesus—the work of telling others the Good News about the wonderful grace of God (Acts 20:24 NLT)

You Can Start Your Life All Over Again

For the older folks reading this, if you are looking back over your life and asking yourself questions like, *What have I done with my life? What have I contributed to humanity? What have I left for the next generation to know that I was here? Have I left footprints in the sands of history?* Do you wish you had a better understanding of vision when you were younger? Do you think you are too old? Some say, *I do not have the energy or time to stir up my gift.*

If you think you are too old to use your gift, you have believed a lie. The internet has marvelous stories of people who have become noteworthy in history because they started all over again when others (even they) thought their lives were almost over. In Proverbs 23:7, King Solomon writes:

For as he thinks in his heart, so *is* he (NKJV).

This was one of Dr. Washington's favourite verses of the Bible. Bill Winston believes that he (Dr. Washington) had a revelation that God made us to function like Him, and that whatever we think on continually we will end up creating. If you convince yourself that you cannot, or allow others to convince you of that, then you will not. On the other hand, if you believe that by God's grace you can, then you will!

Your talents can give you your youth back. They will give you energy and strength. You will be healthier. You will stop talking about dying and start talking about living.

I urge you never to go about feeling shortchanged as though somehow you are lacking. As if you did not get enough, or you cannot do what others can do. Rest assured, you are fully loaded and completely equipped for the race God has designed for you. Be who God created you to be. **You have something unique and powerful to offer the world that nobody else has. You must let your talents shine. You are an authentic masterpiece.**

In the UCB *Word For Today* of Thursday, 25 February 2021, Bob Gass wrote,

Many of us have good ideas that never go anywhere. At some point, you must reduce your list to the best idea for you. This isn't easy but it's necessary. The Bible says, 'Faith without works is dead' (James 2:26 KJV). So commit yourself to a life of creativity, original thinking, and action.! If you keep doing what you've always done, you'll keep getting what you've always got. The classic advertisement for Apple Computer says it best:' 'Think different!' Don't take yourself too seriously! If an idea doesn't work, don't fall apart. Tick it off your list and move on to the next one. At some point, you may discover that your good idea – is actually a God idea. When that happens, it changes everything!

I also want you to draw strength and encouragement from the story of Caleb in Numbers 13 and 14, and Joshua 14:6–15. At eighty-five and against all odds, Caleb believed God's promise and boldly proclaimed, 'Give me this mountain', as the KJV puts it. He steadfastly refused to conform to the majority opinion of fear and unbelief, or become part of a culture of cynicism, self-pity, and recrimination. More impressive still is that he kept his heart hopeful and with a spirit of unstoppable faith. *Give Me This Mountain (Caleb's Song)* by Graham Kendrick is worth listening to. Hear his explanation of the song:

> As often is the case I went through a couple of versions of the song before settling on the final one and honed the words and tune by 'road-testing' it in several live situations. It is proving to be a cry that lots of people identify with, as we face the circumstances that tower above us and seem impossible to conquer until we see how much greater our God is. Caleb received a promise and approval from God: 'But because my servant Caleb has a different spirit and follows me wholeheartedly, I will bring him into the land he went to, and his descendants will inherit it' (Numbers 14:24 NIV), and as the story unfolds this becomes God's verdict on his life-something for all of us to aspire to be: 'wholehearted'.

My prayer is that no matter how severe the life's storms you may be in today, may the Lord help you carry a victorious attitude like Caleb. May you fulfil your destiny in Christ and possess every blessing that God has given you as your inheritance. May you hold on to God's promises, live the life of an overcomer, remain healthy, strong, and youthful all the days of your life. As we all increase in the knowledge of our position and inheritance as children of God, may we rise with boldness to claim the blessings that are rightfully ours in this life and beyond in Jesus's name!

I wrote this chapter to help everyone who belongs to the covenant, the people of destiny, to help them find the right steps to take and identify what motivates them to work out God's divine plan for their lives daily. **Until you discover and fulfill God's purposes for your life, you have not lived at all!**

Behind Every Successful Business, There Is a Story

I was selected to attend an intensive but extremely rewarding *Boost Your Business* course in May 2018 at Ushaw College in Durham, in the North East of England. This was a very high-profile course sponsored jointly by the European Union Skills Funding Agency, North East Enterprise Network, Gateshead College, and New College, Durham. The aim of the course was to develop the attendees' enterprise and entrepreneurial skills to boost their businesses.

As part of the course, the trainers asked each participant to write a story, which would be posted on any social media platform of their choice. My story was something that I was immensely pleased about, and it gave me the highest marks. Within one hour of posting my story on Facebook, I had several likes, wonderful comments, and shares. Here is my story:

My sweet success story

What is today known as *The Best Designer Cakes, Catering and Training Institute* was born out of adversity. I am the CEO and Founder of my confectionery business, only by God's grace. Our products include wedding and other large celebration cakes. I train people in cake making, cake decorating and sugar craft. My company also provides catering services for various functions, including weddings. I can testify that:

> Adversity can be turned to opportunity simply by adjusting our perception and our attitude.   —Gael Lynne Goodwin

> Adversity also has the effect of eliciting talents, which, in prosperous circumstances would have been dormant.   —Horace

Many years ago, I embarked enthusiastically on a master's degree programme in medical microbiology at the university of Newcastle in the North East of England. I was a private student (paying overseas university fees) so I planned to work extremely hard to complete my research laboratory work and write up my thesis in twelve months. I completed my research work successfully in nine months, but for another eighteen months, my supervisor was not available to read and correct my written thesis.

My husband had completed his specialist training in obstetrics and gynaecology and was ready to return to Nigeria to take up a substantive post in one of the teaching hospitals. After prayerfully standing in this severe storm in tears for six months with no change, I did what Elizabeth Edwards said, 'She stood in the storm and when the wind did not blow her away, she adjusted her sails'. Following this example, I quickly adjusted my sails.

I recall waking up one morning in tears indulging in self-pity as I could not imagine returning to Nigeria without my master's degree. Not after the hard work and hefty overseas students' fees paid for a whole academic year. As I sobbed, I heard these words deep down in my spirit, 'Stretch out your hands'. I did so immediately. Again, I heard in my spirit, 'These hands are blessed. Go and put them to use'. Immediately, I knew that God had spoken to me. Deep within me, I knew I had a passion and talent for baking and cooking. These were the two things that were strongly impressed on my mind this morning in question. With this incident firmly in my mind, I went to the bookshop and bought just two books—one on cake making/decorating and the other on cookery. I started trying out recipes on my own from that day.

Over the weeks and months that followed, as I started trying out different recipes in cake making, decorating and sugar craft, and in preparing various dishes, I began to witness the practical expression of the passion and talent that I knew I had. This was how I activated and put to work my cake-making/cake-decorating and culinary talents.

I recall ordering the *Wilton Way of Cake Decorating: Home Study Course* from the United States. By God's grace and with the help of these home study materials, I kept working at this talent—developing and enhancing my own skills. I pay tribute to the significant contribution of my wonderful friend, the late Mrs Aduke Endeley. I got stuck trying to learn a special technique in American cake decorating. She offered to attend a two-week course in the Wilton School of cake decorating in the USA to learn this special technique. On her return, she kindly taught me this new technique. This enhanced my cake decorating skills to a higher level, enabling me to meet more rigorous international standards.

Before long, I was proficient and bold enough to advertise. I did not have a shop, so I worked from home. I put up advertisements on Freeman Hospital notice boards in Newcastle where my husband worked. As time passed, orders started coming in.

Within months, I progressed from an amateur to a competent, confident, and undeniably outstanding specialist cake artist to the glory of God. I must add that my supervisor eventually showed up after eighteen months. What he did not do in eighteen months, he did in two weeks and I finally got my master's degree—glory be to God!

Besides going into cake making/decoration/cookery while waiting for my supervisor, I took a fancy to biomedical science. Shortly after obtaining my master's degree, I was offered a place at the Newcastle General Hospital to train as a biomedical scientist. I successfully completed the Health and Care Professions Council (HCPC)–approved programme in this hospital with special interests in clinical/diagnostic medical microbiology, immunology, and virology. I was now qualified to register as a professional and made an associate of the Institute of Biomedical Science (IBMS) of the UK. I could now practice in the UK if I wanted to, but then my family had to return to Nigeria following the successful completion of my husband's specialist training.

In Nigeria, I took my confectionery business to a different level. I was contracted by leading supermarkets Leventis and Kingsway in Benin City as a major cake supplier. I opened a small training academy and had apprentices who worked with and for me. While all these were going on, the University of Benin Teaching Hospital (UBTH), employed me as a biomedical scientist in the department of microbiology.

When we returned to the UK five years later because my husband was awarded a grant to specialise in another area of medicine, I was upgraded to a Fellow of the Institute of Biomedical Science (IBMS) of the UK. This was because of my ability to show significant career achievement and success, as well as a passion for learning and sharing knowledge.

With this background, I began to lay the foundation for a PhD programme in medical and environmental microbiology and eventually completed it, thank God. At the same time, I continued to run my cake business from home part-time (while also working as a freelance biomedical scientist) until Gateshead Council found me business premises. I combined my secular profession with my cake business and for many years did an excellent job at both. My confectionery business continued to grow.

Today, I am the Chief Executive Officer (CEO) of my company, *The Best Designer Cakes and Training Institute* based at the Blaydon Business Centre in the outskirts of Newcastle upon Tyne in the North East of England. The Mayor, accompanied by officials from Gateshead Council, commissioned my business. It was featured in the Evening Chronicle—a Tyneside newspaper.

My company has trained and produced cake artists both in Nigeria and in the UK. On the 14th of September 2019, the Society Celebration International Celebrity Organisation, accorded me the prestigious award of *The Best Designer Specialist Cake Artist of the Year 2019* during their eminent awards and dinner dance at the Cavendish Banqueting Hall, Colindale, London. In July 2020, the testimony of my work and faith was featured in the 96th edition of their magazine *Society Celebration International Celebrity Journal*. I could not agree more with Albert Einstein that 'Creativity is intelligence having fun'.

One of the best feelings in the world is getting paid to do what you love. I give God all the glory for everything I am and have today. Whatever I will be or have in this life and beyond, it is all by His grace, mercy, and power. PRAISE YAHWEH FOREVERMORE!

Winston Churchill said, 'Success is walking from failure to failure with no loss of enthusiasm'. When I missed out on going into medical school at twenty-one, I promised myself that I would study for a PhD in biological and medical sciences. At forty-two, I finally embarked on my PhD programme. Although the delay was mainly because of family commitments, I have never and will never regret this sacrifice.

I eventually started my long-awaited PhD in the Isle of Man branch of Liverpool University in the department of marine and environmental biology. On the very first day, my supervisor called me to his office to explain why he thought I would fail to deliver on what he described as a very onerous and risky programme. 'I am very concerned about your ability to undertake and complete your PhD programme in what is a very difficult area', he said.

'What are your concerns about my ability to undertake and complete my proposed PhD programme?' I replied, confused.

'Well, I have three main concerns. Firstly, at over forty years of age, it is quite late to be starting something as complex as this. You should not forget you have chosen a very difficult research topic that involves going out to sea to get water samples from different sea depths and samples from under water sewage outfalls. Secondly, you have a husband who works long hours and will need more support than you could give if you started this programme. Lastly, you have three young children who demand time, attention, and have other practical needs that will need to be met'.

I took a moment and replied calmly, 'Thank you for raising your concerns with me. Before applying for this programme, I gave it some serious thought. I know that I am more than capable of doing this well and I know God will help me to do so'.

Following this, he reluctantly allowed me to make a start. After twelve months, he called a meeting to discuss my progress. 'When you were about to embark on your PhD programme, I did not think you would succeed in your pursuit of the programme', he confessed. 'Your results so far have been outstanding, so much so I do not think I am experienced enough in your research area to supervise your work'.

My family was moving to Newcastle upon Tyne after my husband's contract in the Isle of Man ended. So, he arranged for me to transfer to Newcastle University to complete the programme. On arrival, my new supervisor had a different project topic trending. Being a professor of medicine, he wanted us to work on his project together, so we could write as many scientific papers as possible from the study. This work required ground-breaking research. We needed to find a novel approach to the problem, and I had to devise a special technique. I worked night and day for nine months to get it to work.

When the breakthrough was delayed, my supervisor got discouraged, thinking it would never happen. I encouraged him and requested more time to try just one more thing. I sought God's face intensely for a solution, and it happened just at the right time. My supervisor could not believe his eyes. By God's grace and to His glory, I eventually completed my PhD in environmental and medical microbiology at Newcastle University Medical School in my seventh year of part-time study.

My PhD thesis has 457 pages and includes all the work from the Isle of Man and Newcastle universities. My second supervisor at Newcastle university insisted that I include all the work from the Isle of Man department of marine biology because the results were outstanding. The journey was tough and often my studies had to come a distant second to family obligations. I am so grateful to God for making this dream a reality.

From my PhD research, I published two academic books titled:

The Macro and Micro Study of the Environmental Impacts of Sewage Discharges
The Direct Viable Count Methods for Assessing Living Bacterial Numbers in Natural Waters

They showcase my research and expertise in environmental, marine, and medical microbiology and are available on Amazon, eBay, and other academic outlets.

I am deeply honoured and humbled that my books contribute to the ongoing Sanitary Revolution (the introduction of clean water and sewage disposal) chosen by over 11,300 British Medical Journal (BMJ) readers as the most important medical milestone since 1840, when the BMJ was first published. God gets all the glory!

ESSENTIAL POINTS FROM CHAPTER 6

- Taking your faith to your secular job and business should echo or mimic what you do with your faith in church. The only difference is the location.
- Despite everything you do, *you are an ambassador for the kingdom of God in your sphere of influence.*
- Marketplace ministry is not less than pulpit ministry. Serve God in your business and secular employment, not outside them.
- Always bear in mind that when we go to church, hang out with

friends, go to work, take part in meetings, create blueprints, or write a paper, **we are still ambassadors for the King.**

- God established the family as the basic *Ekklesia* through which He would perform His purpose of bringing His kingdom down to earth.
- Until you discover and begin to fulfill God's purposes for your life, you have not lived at all.

Declaration

I am filled and led by the Holy Spirit; therefore, I am successful in all my endeavours. I am anointed of God as a marketplace minister and an ambassador for the kingdom of God in my sphere of influence. The works of my hands are blessed. My business is successful, flourishing through excellence and honesty. I am strong and courageous, making wise decisions, guided by the Holy Spirit. This is my due season year. My vision is so strong that it pulls me to my goals. I am peaceful in my spirit, soul, and body. I am authentic and present. I am a magnet for money and abundance. Love, wisdom, and discernment coexist in my heart. I focus on what God has already done for me. I am a kingdom woman, a splendid wife, parent, leader, entrepreneur, business owner. Success is my duty. My heavenly Father owns the universe and I work for Him. I am taken care of by the King of kings and Lord of lords. I use my wealth and power for the benefit of the kingdom. I always choose the voice of faith and victory. I am blessed beyond imagination and highly favoured. My grand purpose in my business is to give God glory, receive and reflect His love, and act as His agent in bringing benefit to the lives of others. I traverse new rivers, knowing God goes before me. I worship and shout praises, knowing that God paves the way for me. Promotion and elevation shall find me repeatedly. The blessing of the Lord will make me rich with no sorrow. In the rest of this year, I shall be a candidate for uncommon favour and blessing.

I declare this by faith in Jesus's majestic name!

Further Study and Scripture References

Deuteronomy 7:14, 8:18; Psalm 37:4, 84:11; Proverbs 16:3, 23:7, 29:18; Jeremiah 1:5, 29:11; Habakkuk 2:2; Matthew 6:33, 7:7; John 10:10; Romans 8:28; Philippians 1:6, 4:6; 2 Timothy 1:7; James 2:26

CHAPTER 7

Some Personal Stories

The tongue has the power of life and death, and those who love it will eat its fruit (Proverbs 18:21 NIV).

With our words, we speak life or death to situations and also to the spirits of those around us. Our testimonies are not about us, but the power of God at work in our lives. No matter who you are or what you have done or not done, your testimony of God's goodness can bring hope and encouragement to everyone who hears them. Not surprisingly, therefore, the Scripture says:

And they overcame him by the blood of the Lamb, and by the word of their testimony (Revelation 12:11 KJV).

We must use our testimonies to overcome the enemy and help others overcome doubt, anxiety, or fear. Sharing testimonies is also a sure sign that the devil will forever keep losing—hallelujah. It brings hope and encouragement to others, and to yourself as well.

Each time you recount what God has done for you—His protection, preservation, provision, and restoration in diverse ways—it builds your faith, strengthens your connection to Him, and brings confidence in His Word. God is the same yesterday, today, and forever. **If He helped you in the past, He can and will do it again.** So, never underestimate the power of sharing what God has done for you. You may be speaking hope to desperate souls and your testimonies could save a life. If you are alive today, you still have a story to share. It is all about Jesus and His glory, do not make it about yourself. Let us share and build one another up because our testimonies can have a huge impact on other people's lives. Share and see the power that comes when you testify at the right time with pure motives.

> Your story is the key that can unlock someone else's prison. —Anonymous

> What God is bringing you through at this very moment will be the testimony that will bring someone else through. No mess, no message. —Anonymous

> If you give it to God, He transforms your test into a testimony, your mess into a message, and your misery into a ministry. —Anonymous

> The unbelieving world should see our testimony lived out daily because it just may point them to the Savior. —Billy Graham

My Family's Return to the United Kingdom

For God does speak—now one way, now another—though no one perceives it. In a dream, in a vision of the night, when deep sleep falls on people as they slumber on their beds, He may speak in their ears and terrify them with warnings, to turn them from wrongdoing and keep them from pride, to preserve them from the pit, their lives from perishing by the sword (Job 33:14-18 NIV).

My family relocated to Nigeria in August 1983, after five years in Newcastle upon Tyne, UK. My husband had arrived in July 1978 and I joined him in October. Our first two children were born in Newcastle, when my husband was training to become a specialist in obstetrics and gynaecology. As previously mentioned in this book, I did my master's programme in medical microbiology at the medical school of Newcastle

University. Later, I became an Associate of the Institute of Biomedical Science, UK after I satisfied the requirements for membership.

In Nigeria, my husband took up a post at the University of Benin Teaching Hospital (UBTH), first as a senior registrar and later, in December 1983, as a consultant in obstetrics and gynaecology and lecturer in the medical school. His specialist area was pelvic floor problems in women. He also provided services in cancers of women's reproductive systems. Within a few years, it became apparent that there was a vast gap in women's cancer services and a lack of skilled surgical personnel. My husband turned his attention more and more to this area, having gained some experience during his training at the gynaecological cancer centre at the Queen Elizabeth hospital (QEH) in Gateshead, UK. However, he needed more training.

So, the search for a scholarship to return to the UK started. By 1986, he was offered a Commonwealth scholarship. But we turned this down, knowing the stipend would barely support the five of us (we had another baby). Since there was no question of separating the family, we put our faith on the line and trusted God for something better.

Late in 1986, the Royal College of Obstetricians and Gynaecologists (RCOG) advertised the Gladys Dodds Training Fellowship in memory of Gladys Dodds. *Two* fellowships were up for grabs. They reserved one for holders of the membership of the Royal College of Obstetricians and Gynaecologists (MRCOG) practicing in the UK, and the other for holders of MRCOG all over the world. This included members in Canada, Australia, New Zealand, all of Asia including India, Pakistan, Sri Lanka, and Malaysia, and of course the whole of Africa—just *one* fellowship available.

I recall my husband returning from work that afternoon with the advert in his hands. 'Darling, here is an interesting advert, but we will have to stretch our faith as far as it can go to believe God', he said.

'GO FOR IT, darling', I replied, without batting an eyelid. He applied for the scholarship, aware that his chance was extremely slim. We prayed about it from time to time, but just refused to think about that application in the natural.

Sometime in 1987, I had a dream. My husband and I worked in UBTH, Benin City in different departments. We usually met for lunch and maybe a stroll. In this dream, I saw myself walk up to my husband's office, as usual at lunchtime. As I was getting ready to return to my department afterwards, he said, 'Darling, do not leave just yet, let us have a short stroll outside my office'.

'Okay darling', I replied. As we walked, he put one hand in his pocket and handed me a brown official envelope. I opened the envelope and screamed with excitement, then I woke up. I could not make sense of this dream. I share virtually everything with my husband, but for some reason, I did not share this with him. Busy with life, I forgot about the dream.

A few weeks later, I walked up to my husband's office that unforgettable afternoon. After lunch, as I was getting ready to go, my husband said: 'Darling, do not leave just yet, let us have a short stroll outside my office'.

I just said, 'Okay, darling'. As we walked, he put one hand in his pocket and handed me a brown official envelope. I opened the envelope and screamed with excitement—**just like the dream.** The envelope contained a letter from the RCOG informing him they had awarded him the **one** Gladys Dodds Fellowship open for all holders of MRCOG outside the UK.

Immediately, I remembered that dream. That astounded me—it all happened *exactly* as I was shown. Over thirty-three years gone, and that dream is still indelible in my mind. How awesome our God is! By God's grace, I have received revelations in dreams ever since—praise God forevermore!

But how could this scholarship happen? Just one chance in several hundred or even thousands. The Gladys Dodds scholarship was more generous than the Commonwealth scholarship we turned down and would sustain our family while my husband trained in Glasgow. This was how we returned to the UK in 1988. Our God is great!

A prophet's confirmation of my gift of dreaming

I am grateful to God for my wonderful, God-fearing husband, the father of our highly favoured and blessed children. He is endowed with a massive understanding of his role as the father and priest of his household. He always wanted to raise kingdom children. This desire increased as he grew in the wisdom and knowledge of God over the years. When our children were growing up, he formed the habit of taking the family to Christian conferences in the summer. We enjoyed going to the New Wine festivals, Dales Bible week, and Kenneth Copeland conferences in various cities in the UK.

Something remarkable happened at a meeting of the New Wine conference in Shepton Mallet. Shepton Mallet is a delightful English town in Somerset, eighteen miles south of Bristol. My husband and I sat in the first morning meeting this beautiful day. Suddenly, the American guest speaker, James Ryle, a renowned prophet of God, said, 'The Lord has a word for a couple here'. He then politely asked my husband and I to stand. Before I continue with my story, I must say that this man of God is one of the most humble and true prophets I have ever met. He started to prophesy over us. He began by recounting some of the things the Lord had recently accomplished in our lives and what He was doing and what His plans were for our near future. How could a prophecy be so accurate, we wondered?

He concluded by saying that the Lord gives me revelations in dreams and that anointing would increase. Because the first part of his prophecies regarding our past and present were so accurate, we were inclined to believe his prophecies concerning our future. By God's grace, my gift of dreaming has been validated over the years.

God did it again and took us to another level

My husband concluded his training in gynaecological cancer just as his scholarship ended. He was now in need of a steady, well-paid job to sustain the family. While waiting for that, he engaged in short-term locum jobs. God also provided a job for me as a biomedical scientist at the Stobhill Hospital in Glasgow. When my husband worked away, I was left with three young children, still doing a stressful full-time job. Life was tough. I recall one of the consultant microbiologists in my department would offer to do some afternoon school runs for me just to take the pressure off. God can use anybody to bless His children. May the Lord remember this man and his family for good. Day and night, I prayed for a good job for my husband where the family would be together. I believe God dropped this verse of Scripture in my spirit:

> But my God shall supply all your need according to His riches in glory by Christ Jesus (Philippians 4:19 KJV).

I confessed it incessantly, daily, while awaiting a miracle of an extraordinary job for my husband. Just another job would not suffice, I was believing for something extraordinary.

An exceptional job

During a locum assignment in Newcastle upon Tyne, my husband phoned one afternoon to say he found an interesting advert in the British Medical Journal (BMJ) for a locum consultant post at the Nobles hospital in the Isle of Man. 'Where is the Isle of Man located?' I asked.

'A tiny island in the Irish Sea between Great Britain and Ireland', he explained. 'But *today* is the last day to apply. I have only a couple of hours to do so', he quickly added.

I encouraged him to apply. He did and faxed his application immediately. Long story short, he got the job, praise God!

This was not just a consultant post but an outstanding one with incredible benefits. God moved our family to this beautiful island. I reserve the story of our stay in the Isle of Man for another book. The years we spent on this amazing island have been the best part of our lives so far. God in His mercy did some extraordinary things for us during our stay there. This was where I eventually embarked on my dream PhD programme after twenty-one years. This was where I was asked by the women in our local church to start and lead the first women's group. We still have fond memories of our time on this beautiful island and wish to visit as often as possible.

Deportation Order

Before we moved to the Isle of Man, my husband started applying to the UK Home Office for indefinite leave to remain. We handed our case over to solicitors in London. We believed they were negotiating with the Home Office until June 30, 1991, when our visas expired. We attended hearings in Glasgow and Tribunal appeals in London. Each time, our case was knocked back and rejected. Finally, early in 1992, we received a deportation order from the Home Office to leave the Isle of Man and not return to any part of the British Isles. What were we to do? We prayed to our God, the Possessor of the ends of the earth, and trusted Him for a breakthrough. We also enlisted the help of a member of the Isle of Man Parliament and a Member of Parliament (MP) from Northern Ireland, to no avail. My husband, myself, our children, and some close Christian friends continued to seek God for a breakthrough.

While we were still praying, we got a second deportation order, and they fixed a date for our removal. We did not budge. We did not pack our belongings. We did not prepare to move. Come the appointed day, we were not surprised when the officials did not turn up. Not the next day, next week, or next month. My husband's contract on the Isle of Man was ending. He looked for a substantive post in the UK as such an appointment would invariably attract a visa. His experiences with short listing and interviews are another story.

God eventually provided another long-term locum consultant post in Hexham, Northumberland. Hexham hospital was part of the large group of Newcastle upon Tyne hospitals. Upon appointment, we retrieved our passports from our solicitors in September 1993, and to our horror, the last visa stamp was valid only until June 30, 1991.

The personnel department at the Newcastle Hospital sent off our passports for visas to enable my husband start work. To our amazement, our passports came back within two weeks with visas approved and stamped for three years. Remember, there was an unexplained gap of two years. There were no questions from the same Home Office who issued the deportation order. Today we are British citizens and carry British passports—glory to God!

Restoration of My Licence to Practice as a Biomedical Scientist

After I got my PhD, I worked full time at the Royal Victoria Infirmary (RVI) in Newcastle upon Tyne. I later resigned to freelance. That meant I chose the location and duration of any contracts. My work took me to various hospitals in the UK, the Republic of Ireland, and the Channel Islands.

I recall a nasty experience in one hospital I worked in, in the UK. That I dared complain about the mistreatment I suffered from some colleagues was offensive to them, and especially to my boss. They fabricated a long list of allegations against me. They reported me to our professional body, the Institute of Biomedical Science (IBMS). My accusers insisted my name be struck off the professional register and my license to practice in the UK be withdrawn.

To add insult to injury, even before the professional body heard my side of the story, they concluded that they would find me guilty and said so in a letter to me! Unbelievable! We shared this with a close friend who advised us to take the letter to our MP. We declined because we knew we were not wrestling against flesh and blood. Instead, my husband and I stood our ground in the spirit's realm, wielding the weapons of our warfare that are not carnal but mighty through God to the pulling down of strongholds (See 2 Corinthians 10:3-4).

My plaintiffs summoned me to a tribunal in London. For months, I sought for a solicitor to handle my case, to no avail. My husband and I just kept crying out to God night and day for His intervention. Miraculously, two weeks before the hearing, the Lord provided a solicitor who introduced us to a barrister. The barrister was so troubled when he heard my story and the injustice meted out to me. He said to my husband and me, 'There is so much injustice at play here. I am going to see that this case is not even opened at the tribunal because *you have no case to answer*. All I ask for is that you pray for me'. Those words were so comforting. We did just that and went to the tribunal.

Not only were my accusers denied entry to the tribunal before my barrister made his recommendation, but he also insisted that I had no case to answer and gave his reasons. After his opening arguments, the legal team advising the tribunal chairman excused themselves to confer with the plaintiffs. I can only imagine the confusion God set in their midst.

The team returned to the courtroom with drawn faces. Their lead solicitor apologised profusely for the inconvenience they caused me by *dragging* me to the tribunal when I had no case to answer. They threw my case out in fifty-five minutes. Before we left our hotel room that morning, my husband and I held hands and he declared that the hearing would not last more than one hour. That was exactly what happened. My barrister got the chairman of my professional association to sign an undertaking that they would never harass me or resurrect that case in the future.

To God's glory, IBMS renewed my licence to practice less than one week after my appearance at the tribunal. I know friends, some solicitors, doctors, and others whose names have been struck off their professional registers and their licences to practice withdrawn. Many committed minor and pardonable mistakes, while others did nothing wrong like in my case. If you are a victim of injustice, I encourage you to forgive and let God be your vindicator! It is a cruel world, but our God reigns!

God's Healing Power

I have many testimonies of God's healing power in my family. I will share only one and reserve the others for another book.

About thirteen years ago, I had what I thought were symptoms of a chest infection (scary palpitations, serious chest pain, and breathlessness). I prayed and ignored them, hoping the symptoms would abate with time, but they got worse. I finally gave in and went to see my General Practitioner (GP). Before that visit, I had not visited the practice for years because the Lord kept me in excellent health. My work as a freelance biomedical scientist took me to various places within and outside the United Kingdom. I was very energetic, full of vigour, and in vibrant health.

My GP examined me, and from her countenance, I guessed there was a problem. She informed me I had a heart murmur and needed to see a cardiologist immediately. I tried to explain to her there was no hurry, but this concerned doctor would not listen. Right before my eyes, she picked up the phone and started making the arrangements.

I was so shocked and in total disbelief. Where did this come from, I asked? On my return home, I shared my experience with my husband. I asked him to listen to my heart with his stethoscope as I wanted a second opinion. His finding was even more revealing and shocking. My husband, who is not easily moved by life's battles, was alarmed and said, 'This is not just a heart murmur, but a very loud one. But we shall overcome'.

I realised there was a serious problem and I would need to fight for my life. Once we got over the initial shock, we rejected both the GP's and my husband's clinical findings. We decided to believe God's report instead and stretch our faith in His Word as far as it could go.

My cardiologist arranged an electrocardiogram (ECG). The initial result was terrible and worrying. My husband and I acknowledged the report but refused to accept it as the ultimate word. A more detailed and sophisticated echocardiogram (ECHO) was arranged. It confirmed the initial result consistent with a rare heart condition.

The way my cardiologist explained it, it felt like a death sentence. If you have never received a death sentence, it is pretty emotional—no matter how spiritual you think you are. We again acknowledged what the specialist had said, but once more rejected it as the final verdict.

They alerted the regional hospital of this finding, and they sent officials to further investigate and store my blood samples in the national archive and carry out genetic studies. I declined and refused to allow anyone to take more blood. They put me on some heart medication, which I took as directed by my cardiologist. We kept crying out to the Lord and kept binding and losing.

I formed the habit of praying at midnight and made a collection of healing Scriptures which I fed my spirit night and day. I listened to Kenneth Hagin's and Gloria Copeland's healing messages several times a day. I also listened to healing praise and confessions by Kenneth and Gloria Copeland. I read the testimonies of God's healing power in the lives of other people. I used Charles Capps's and Elisha Goodman's healing manuals. I took communion virtually every day.

After several days, my husband and I began to experience God's peace. How wonderful it was for us. When you have the triune God and His Word, you can come to a place of peace even during the most ferocious storms of life. The more we studied and confessed the Word of God over my body, the more our faith in His healing power took hold in our hearts.

My husband and I kept this health challenge between us and the Lord. We did not even share it with our children because we did not wish to frighten them. My cardiologist did not think I should be working, but I refused to give up my job. Not only was I working, but I was doing so at the West Suffolk Hospital in Bury St Edmunds, many miles away from my home in Newcastle. Working here meant leaving by train every Sunday evening, and returning home on Friday night.

My cardiologist also advised me to avoid taking the stairs. My flat in Bury St Edmunds was on the third floor and the building had no lift. That meant taking the stairs at least six times a day, as I spent my lunch breaks in my flat, just a stone's throw from my office.

At some point, I just knew that I knew that I knew that the Lord is big and faithful enough to restore my health. Jesus had already paid a costly price for our healing and redeemed us from the curse of the law according to Galatians 3:13 and 14. God not only laid our iniquities upon Jesus, but our diseases as well. Jesus was born to bear our sin, and sicknesses/diseases. And if they were borne by Him, then, it is wrong for us to bear them.

He was despised and rejected and forsaken by men, a Man of sorrows and pains, and acquainted with grief and sickness; and like One from Whom men hide their faces He was despised, and we did not appreciate His worth or have any esteem for Him.

Surely He has borne our griefs (sicknesses, weaknesses, and distresses) and carried our sorrows and pains [of punishment], yet we [ignorantly] considered Him stricken, smitten, and afflicted by God [as if with leprosy].

But He was wounded for our transgressions, He was bruised for our guilt and iniquities; the chastisement [needful to obtain] peace and well-being for us was upon Him, and with the stripes [that wounded] Him we are healed and made whole (Isaiah 53:3–5 AMPC).

Through the ministry of Jesus on earth, God our Father revealed that it was His will to heal man physically. In redemption, God broke the power of disease over man and set him free by laying our disease and sickness over Christ.

I allowed this simple truth to settle in my heart by meditating on it, speaking it over and over to myself until it registered in my spirit. I then weaned myself off medication and was led to share this health challenge with a dear and trusted friend, professor Ene Ette (an anointed Marketplace minister, clinical pharmacologist, and chief executive officer of Anoixis corporation based in Boston, United States). A Bible teacher with a massive understanding of the Word of God, he ministers the Word in the power of the Holy Spirit, with signs and wonders following.

He assured me of my victory in Christ Jesus. He prayed with me over the phone and rebuked that heart condition. My husband and I stood against that condition and stubbornly refused to accept or believe the doctors' reports as final concerning my health. My cardiologist tried to make me accept what the results suggested, but I politely refused without going into any arguments with him. I knew Whom I had believed and stood my ground.

It was now time for my next appointment with the cardiologist. I asked for a repeat ECHO and he agreed. The technician assured that the repeat examination would take a maximum of thirty minutes, but forty-five minutes in, the specialist performing the ECHO requested the help of a more senior and experienced specialist. About one hour and fifteen minutes later, they sent for the most experienced ECHO technician who did the initial thorough examination that led to the diagnosis. The three technicians looked confused and puzzled.

I had been in the examination room for over one and a half hours and was getting concerned about the penalty for overstaying in the hospital car park. 'Excuse me please, is there a problem?' I asked.

'No, there is no problem', she replied.

'Why then have you sent for two other colleagues to be involved in my examination?' I probed.

'I want a second opinion about the result of my current investigation. There seems to be a significant difference between the results today and those of your first ECHO', she explained. 'This is the reason I have invited my senior colleague who performed your first examination. Your medication is doing an excellent job'.

She continued, 'We cannot reconcile our findings today with the previous. There is an obvious discrepancy between the first and second ECHO results. However, you will need to see your cardiologist as soon as possible'.

At my next visit, my cardiologist had the two ECHO results in front of him. He looked stumped. To confirm the report, he arranged for a computerised tomography (CT) scan. My husband accompanied me to the clinic this time round. Looking more confused and embarrassed than ever, the cardiologist told us he could not explain the sudden change in their findings.

His report to my GP, which was also sent to me, is worth quoting to some extent: 'I reviewed Mrs. Betty Nwabineli in my clinic today. Previously, there had been discrepancies in the two echocardiograms on separate occasions regarding left ventricular outflow tract (LVOT) gradients. . . . However, a CT scan has shown no evidence of LVOT obstruction'. He concluded it was a wrong diagnosis. My cardiologist struck off the previous report from my records in my presence. He advised me to ask my insurance company to contact him should I ever have any problems with home or life insurance. He discharged me from his clinic straightaway. To the glory of God, this was over thirteen years ago. All the symptoms disappeared, never to return, in Jesus's majestic and victorious name—hallelujah!

I can testify that God in His mercy and power intervened in my situation, turned my mourning into dancing and my sorrow into joy, hallelujah! The bottom line is that **God still heals today** regardless of the sickness, disease, or condition. To Him alone be all the glory and honour forever and ever, amen! **No matter what the challenge may be (health, finances, jobs, relationships, etc), fixing your eyes on the Word of God and meditating on it will always cause you to be victorious**.

For I will restore health to you, and your wounds I will heal, declares the Lord, because they have called you an outcast: It is Zion, for whom no one cares! (Jeremiah 30:17 ESV).

My son, attend to my words; consent and submit to my sayings. Let them not depart from your sight; keep them in the centre of your heart. For they are life to those who find them, healing and health to all their flesh. Keep and guard your heart with all vigilance and above all that you guard, for out of it flows the springs of life (Proverbs 4:20–23 AMPC).

God Speaks in a Still Small Voice

... for He [God] himself has said, I will not in any way fail you nor give you up nor leave you without support. [I will] not, [I will] not, [I will] not in any degree leave you helpless nor forsake nor let [you] down (relax my hold on you)! [assuredly not!] (Hebrews 13:5 AMPC).

I recall one unforgettable afternoon. I had been ministering to a depressed and distressed friend and I took her shopping. I had no cash, so I had to stop at the ATM. I put the notes in my purse and tucked my purse away in my handbag securely hung on my shoulder. My friend and I walked into a popular supermarket in the shopping centre.

Unknown to me, a thief who saw me withdraw money from the ATM trailed us into the supermarket. Oblivious, I heard a still small voice in my spirit suddenly urge me to look in my handbag. Why examine my bag, I wondered? I ignored the first two prompts. Then came an extraordinarily powerful urge to check my handbag. Although it was not an audible voice, it sounded like one in my spirit. I immediately recognised the voice—it was undeniably the voice of the Lord. When I eventually examined my handbag, I got a rude shock. My purse, containing all the money I had just withdrawn, together with all my bank cards and other sensitive items, had disappeared. How could that be when I had my handbag hung over my right shoulder? It would amaze you how skilled thieves are in doing their dirty work. But the Lord was with me, fulfilling His promise in the above Scripture, even though I was not praying at the time—how comforting!

As soon as I discovered the disappearance of my purse, I raised the alarm right there. I kept screaming so loudly that everything in that area came to a standstill. I insisted that someone in the shop had snatched my purse from my handbag. Some people rebuked me for accusing anyone in the shop of stealing my purse. But like blind Bartimaeus in Mark 10:46–52, I shouted all the more. I just knew that I knew that the thief was still in the store. I kept on screaming and ignored everyone, including my mentee (who was beyond mortified).

Suddenly, I felt an urge in my spirit to hush. It appeared as if I was now in the spirit and taking instructions from an unseen Being. The instructions were extremely specific and compelling, but also risky and *scary*. The first instruction was: 'Go straight to the guy standing over there right in front of you and retrieve your purse'. I had no time to think, question, or rationalise. This thief could have easily sneaked out of the supermarket while all this was going on. But the fear of God froze him so much, he could not move. He just backed himself to a wall and stood still like a statue.

Meanwhile, angry shoppers were standing around, watching me. It looked like a movie.

I walked straight up to this guy: 'You've got my purse'.

'What?' he replied.

'Shut up', I responded. He did and raised both hands in total surrender. Still following the instructions of that glorious still small voice, I put my hand in the precise pocket in his jacket and pulled out my purse—intact, nothing missing.

You should have heard the roar of the spectators who had been watching me in wonder and amazement. During the commotion that followed, the thief took to his heels and disappeared. I suddenly returned to myself, like someone who had just woken up from a dream. I could not even believe what had just taken place.

Again, like the many who rebuked Bartimaeus, the same people who rebuked me when I raised the alarm were quick to rush over, asking, 'How did you know he was the thief, after all, he was not the only man in the store?' I had no answer for them, instead, I raised my hands in praise and worship.

Then my relieved mentee said, 'Our God is great'. This experience emboldened this lady into shameless evangelism. The enemy's plan to disgrace me and discourage her rebounded, should I say *boomeranged* seriously. This is one of the sweetest triumphs God has performed in my life. This episode significantly encouraged the faith of my mentee and propelled her to another level in her walk with God. She has never looked back since then. Praise God forevermore.

The supermarket manager would not let me go

On my way back to my car, the supermarket manager ran up to me. 'Excuse me please, can I request your contact details for the police?'

'There is no need because I have forgiven the thief', I responded.

'I have been the manager of this store for years and have never seen a thing like this before. We must report this incident to the police', he pleaded. I yielded and passed on my contact details.

Two police officers came to my home afterwards. After giving my statement, they were still surprised. They said they had been in the police force for several years and had never once heard anything like that. They insisted on knowing how I knew it was that guy who stole my purse. I shared my experience, but as the Scripture says:

> But the natural [unbelieving] man does not accept the things [the teachings and revelations] of the Spirit of God, for they are foolishness [absurd and illogical] to him; and he is incapable of understanding them, because they are spiritually discerned and appreciated, [and he is unqualified to judge spiritual matters] (1 Corinthians 2:14 AMP).

'How can we too be empowered to catch thieves?' they inquired. That gave my husband and I the opportunity to deposit the seed of the gospel in their hearts.

'You have to be filled with the Holy Spirit', my husband responded.

'Would you like to work with the local police force to help in catching thieves?' they asked.

'Of course not', I responded.

Miracles that ensued after I shared this testimony

Jersey General Hospital in St Helier in the Channel Island had contracted me to work in the department of microbiology for several months. This meant catching a flight to Jersey on Sunday evenings, working all week, and catching a flight home after work on Fridays. At that time, I was the OFNC (Overseas Fellowship of Nigerian Christians) National Women's Coordinator. My responsibilities included coordinating the national women's conferences and visiting various women's groups to minister to precious daughters of God.

One weekend, I caught a flight on a Friday evening and had to travel the next day to minister in the London branch of the OFNC Women's Fellowship. I had had no time to prepare properly. While on the train to London, I told the Lord I was not sure what to share. I felt the Lord say: 'Relax, just share the testimony of how you caught the thief in the supermarket'. Although I did not quite understand how such a testimony would impact anyone, I received the instruction. It turned out to be a big meeting. I shared my testimony, had a glorious time with the ladies, and returned to Newcastle. The leader of the group later informed me that many who attended the fellowship that day shared my testimony with their families to the glory of God.

First miracle

A few weeks later, I got an interesting phone call from the leader of the London Women's Fellowship. She informed me that a lady who heard my testimony had her purse stolen from her pocket. This happened while she was alighting from a coach at Elephant and Castle station in southeast London. Remembering my story made her resolve not to be shy or embarrassed to raise the alarm. She did, and the police rushed to the scene immediately. To her surprise, her purse was recovered intact from a fellow passenger who travelled on the same coach. God is good!

Second miracle: a little boy's faith

Another lady who attended the same meeting told the story to her family when she got home. Her thirteen-year-old son, who was in Year 9 at the time, heard how God led me to catch the thief in the supermarket.

He had been preparing for an examination and stored his work on a memory stick. He slipped it in his pocket and lost it during a school coach trip. The next day, he realised he had lost all his project data. He was devastated, but his faith was stirred up when he remembered my testimony. He told his family, 'The God Who helped auntie Betty catch that thief in the supermarket will help me find my memory stick'. He stood by those words. With every assurance he would recover the memory stick, they started praying and searching. Long story short, they led him to the coach driver who took them on the school trip days before. He was not surprised at all when the coach driver said they found a memory stick on the coach and kept it in a safe place. It turned out to be the one he was looking for—praise God. Perhaps this thirteen-year-old boy would have lost his work if his mum had not been to that meeting and if I had not shared my testimony—glory to God!

....

ESSENTIAL POINTS FROM CHAPTER 7

- God still speaks to us in dreams, even today.
- God still heals today. It is His will to heal the human body.
- In redemption, we have been bought back, brought back, and set free from the curse of the law.

Declaration

I plant the seed of God's Word in my heart. I continue to water that seed and, eventually, I will see a harvest of health and healing. Because my disease and sickness were laid upon Jesus Christ, I am healed and set free. I accept as truth that Jesus bore my disease and sickness. I boldly confess that I am healed and made whole. I speak the Word of

God. I speak faith-filled, life-filled words that change the circumstances around me. I refuse to speak doubt and unbelief.

I declare this by faith in Jesus's majestic name!

Further Study and Scripture References

Job 33:14; Psalm 30:2, 103:3, 107:20; Isaiah 53:3–5,10; Jeremiah 30:17; 1 Peter 2:24.

Conclusion

Now all has been said, what is the conclusion of the matter? I aim to challenge and redirect kingdom women to God's original intent for women in society. The contents of this book are backed up by Scriptures and the wisdom and experience of anointed godly men and women who are gifted in these areas.

If after reading this book, you are stirred up to take stock of where you have been and where you are now, and you then decide where you want to be and how you might get there in the fulfilment of God's call on your precious life, then for me, this book has been a success.

I have drawn from my own experiences on how I got to know God. Embracing Jesus Christ as a teenager remains the best and most important decision I ever made. While kingdom people have different gifts, the need to understand God's unique call on our lives cannot be overemphasised. The highest call ever is to be conformed to the image of Jesus Christ. Have you embraced this?

Following my mother's example, I have determinedly tried to model my life after the Proverbs 31 woman. The excellence of this virtuous woman focuses on who she is. She lives a life of excellence with purpose, diligence, and freedom. A kingdom woman who is constantly yielded and sensitive to the Holy Spirit can become a spiritual 360-degree woman, complete in all dimensions—social, physical, mental, and spiritual. Such a woman will be an excellent wife, mother, entrepreneur, and a marketplace minister. Because she has an unbroken relationship with God, she builds capacity in herself. When a woman builds capacity in herself, she is building capacity in the family, and when she builds capacity in the family, she is building capacity in the nation. Are you such a kingdom woman? If not, what will you do differently henceforth to become one?

Excellence is a kingdom hallmark. It is God's very nature. God's perfect will is that His people prize excellence.

I have made a passionate appeal for excellence in all that kingdom people do; and for married kingdom women to put their families first, irrespective of what they do outside the home. I have also traced parts of my journey through life looking at a kingdom woman first as a single person, later as a wife (homemaker), mother (parent), grandmother, medical microbiologist/biomedical scientist, entrepreneur, and a marketplace minister.

Of course, these roles are not necessarily compartmentalised, or, for that matter, sequential. They overlap and, in many instances, occur concurrently. For clarity and emphasis, these roles have been examined and dealt with in different chapters. This has been done deliberately in order to allow time and space for detail and to base the story on Scripture (which is infallible) so that we all can explore the mind of God in these areas.

Personal testimonies and those of family and friends provide true-life realities that we can all relate to. Quotes from anointed men and women of God as well as well-known philosophers, bloggers, and writers complement the story. The result, I hope, is that the contents of the book are not so *heavenly* upward that they become beyond reach and appear unattainable, or on the other hand so earthly bound that the salt loses its saltiness.

The Kingdom Woman as an Excellent Homemaker (Chapter 3) and *The Kingdom Woman as an Excellent Wife* (Chapter 4) are especially important in the life and ministry of any Christian woman. Just as important is *The Kingdom Woman as an Excellent Parent* (Chapter 5). From a biblical perspective, the mission of kingdom parents is to raise godly children. To that end, God designed the family as the primary unit by which children are loved, trained, and empowered. The chapter on raising godly generations explains how successful parenting provokes God's generational blessings on families and fulfils the thinking of the Godhead in creating man in the first instance.

Through childbearing, God fully desires to reproduce Himself and by the effect of godly parenting ensure that Christ would become replicated all over the world. As a kingdom parent, do you think of your responsibilities in these terms?

Family is very important to God. It is the foundation of the church and society. Where the family fails, society descends into chaos as evident in many societies around the world today. Therefore, the chapter on parenthood and leaving a godly legacy goes into significant detail on practical steps to raise godly children. As well as the dos, there is also in-depth discussion about the don'ts. This chapter also explains the five-generation rule. How a parent raises their child/children—the love, values, emotional environment, and education they provide—influences not only their children, but the four generations to follow, either for good or evil.

It is especially important to remember that the Bible does not reserve motherhood only for women with biological children. Judges 5 identifies the prophet and judge Deborah as a mother in Israel, but she was also a mother to Israel. She provided wisdom and showed Israel the way to go. She even tried to encourage her grown child to follow God on his own, without her constant presence. Because of Deborah's wisdom and guidance, Israel enjoyed a rare period of peace. All women can follow Deborah's example to encourage, nurture, and train those around them to live mature, effective, and God-honouring lives.

I have discussed the kingdom woman as an entrepreneur and a marketplace minister using the Proverbs 31 woman and successful New Testament businesswomen such as Priscilla and Lydia as examples. The understanding of marketplace ministry should encourage kingdom women that performing their duties as singles, wives, mothers, entrepreneurs, marketplace ministers, and pulpit ministers constitutes their full-time ministry callings.

As a kingdom citizen, it is crucial that you devote serious, focused time and effort into working out a clear picture of where you are going in life. Consider the poignant words of the Apostle Paul who had no regrets even when he knew that his death was near. Having lived his life with great passion and dedication to the Lord, he was confident that he had fulfilled his calling. What about you? Have you found your purpose in life? You must find your purpose, your God-given assignment, and pursue it with passion.

Although the book is primarily addressed to kingdom women, it contains nuggets that everyone can learn from. I have also encouraged and challenged kingdom husbands to love their wives as the Word of God commands and to live with them in knowledge and harmony.

If this book inspires you to pursue kingdom excellence in all areas of your life, with the realisation that every kingdom person can become all that God designed them to be, then it has fulfilled its purpose.

Notes

NOTES TO CHAPTER 2

Excellence: *The American Heritage Dictionary of the English Language.* Boston: Houghton Mifflin, 2000.

Arete (Greek ἀρετή): *Strong's Concordance 703.*

M.S. Rao: *Strive for Excellence, Not Perfection.* https://www.oreilly.com/library/view/21-success sutras/9788131795750/xhtml/chapter006.xhtml

Oknéros (Greek ὀκνηρός): *Strong's Concordance 3836.*

Achreios (Greek ἀχρεῖος): *Strong's Concordance 888.*

Christian Baker: http://christianbaker.net/blog/repeatedly/.

Anthony Robbins: https://goodreads.com/quotes/328976-it-s-not-what-we-do-once-in-a-while-that.

Thomas J. Peters: *In Search of Excellence: Lessons From America's Best-Run Companies.* www.researchgate.net › 20705258-Thomas-J-Peters.

Caelan Huntress and Frank Herron: *Excellence is a Habit: 7 Lessons from This Aristotle Quote.* www.developgoodhabits.com › excellence-habit.

Dr. Myles Munroe: *Understanding the Purpose and Power of Women: God's Design for Female Identity.*

Scott Gross: *Positively Outrageous Service. How to delight and astound your customers and win them for life.* p. 8.

Rakesh and Kirti Seth: *Creating customer delight: the how and why of CRM.* p. 19.

Celestine Chua: *10 Steps To Achieve Excellence in Anything—Life Optimizer.* https//www.lifeoptimizer.org/2009/09/04/steps-to-achieve-excellence/.

NOTES TO CHAPTER 3

Dictionary.com: *Housewife*. https://www.dictionary.com/browse/housewife.
Oxford Dictionary: *Housewife*. https://www.lexico.com/definition/housewife.
Merriam-Webster: *Housewife*. https://www.merriam-webster.com/dictionary/housewife.
The British Chambers' Twentieth Century Dictionary (1901): *Housewife*. https://en.wikipedia.org/wiki/Chambers_Dictionary.
Dictionary.com: *Homemaker*. https://www.dictionary.com/browse/homemaker.
Lexico.Com: *Homemaker*. https://www.lexico.com/definition/homemaker.
Merriam-Webster: *Homemaker*. https://www.merriam-webster.com/dictionary/homemaker.
Collins Dictionary: *Homemaker*. https://www.collinsdictionary.com/dictionary/english/homemaker.
Oikouros: *Strong's Concordance* 3626.
Titus 2 Commentary: *Vincent's Word Studies*. https://www.studylight.org/commentaries/eng/vnt/titus-2.html.
Stephen Armstrong: *What Does the Bible Say About Mothers Working Outside the Home?* https://www.versebyverse ministry.org/bible-answers/should-christian-mothers-work.
Dennis and Barbara Rainey: *Starting Your Marriage Right: What You Need to Know in the Early Years to Make It Last a Lifetime.* p. 126.
Lauren Eberspacher: *Is It a Sin to Be a Christian Woman and Work Outside the Home?* https://herviewfromhome.com/is-it-a-sin-to-be-a-christian -woman -and-work-outside-the-home/.
Marg Mowczko: *Busy at Home: How Does Titus 2:4-5 Apply Today?* https://margmowczko.com/busy-at-home-how-does-titus-24-5-apply-today/.
Francis Bacon (1605): *Where Does 'Cleanliness Next To Godliness' Phrase Come From?* https://ambotv.com/blog/where-does-cleanliness-next-to-godliness -phrase-come-from/.
John Wesley: *The Phrase Finder:'Cleanliness is next to Godliness'.* https://www.phrases.org.uk/meanings/cleanliness-is-next-to-godliness.html.
Romeo Vitelli: *Is Doing Housework a Turn-On? New research on whether couples who share the load spend more time in bed.* https://www.psychologytoday.com/us/blog/media-spotlight/201603/is-doing-housework-turn.
Matthew D. Johnson, Nancy L. Galambos, and Jared R Anderson: *Skip the dishes? Not so fast! Sex and housework revisited.* https://pubmed.ncbi.nlm.nih.gov/26461485/.
British Medical Journal: *The Introduction of Clean Water And Sewage Disposal.* https://www.bmj.com/content/334/7585/111.2.

NOTES TO CHAPTER 4

Dorothy Patterson: *The High Calling of Wife and Mother in Biblical Perspective*. https://bible.org/seriespage/high-calling-wife-and-mother-biblical-perspective.
Dorothy Morrison: *My Turn*, p. 14.

NOTES TO CHAPTER 4

Hupotasso: *Strong's Concordance* 5293.
Marg Mowczko: *Abigail: A Bible Woman with Beauty and Brains*. https://margmowczko.com/abigail-1-samuel-25/.
Denise Renner: *28-Day Journey. Day 26: Lessons from Abigail*. https://renner.org/article/day-26-lessons-from-abigail/.
Mackintosh W. Mackay: *The Woman of Tact, and Other Bible Types of Modern Women*. New York and London: Hodder and Stroughton, 1912. xiii, 328 p.
Abigail—*Loving Gospel*. https://www.lovinggospel.com/Abigail.htm.
Jerome Blanco: *Abigail: The Peacemaker*. https://depree.org/abigail-the-peacemaker/.
Phyllis Bird: *Women as Agents of Salvation in the Old Testament*.
Max Lucado: *Ten Women Who Changed the Bible: One By One They Changed the World*. p. 70.

NOTES TO CHAPTER 5

Jennifer Alden: *The Joy Of Motherhood—'Godly Mothers Are The Nation's Greatest Treasure*. https://godtv.com/the-joy-of-motherhood/.
Thomas Nelson Bibles: *A Noble Ministry*. https://www.thomasnelsonbibles.com/motherhood-a-noble-ministry/.
Klēsis (Greek κλῆσις): *Strong's Concordance* 2821.
Tony Evans: *One Family Under God*.
Daniel Whitworth: *Will Your Children Go to Heaven?* https://www.biblesaints.com/resources/articles/2016/03/21/will-your-children-go-to-heaven.
Jennifer Newton: *Air Traffic Control in the UK Had its Busiest Year Ever in 2019*. https://www.dailymail.co.uk/travel/travel_news/article-8073381/Air-traffic-control-UK-busiest-year-2019-handling-2-6million-flights.html.
E. Winship: *Jukes-Edwards: A Study in Education and Heredity. https://www.uknewman.com/portfolio-items/family-comparisons-december-30-2018/*.
A.E. Winship: *Litt.D: .Jukes And Edwards*. https://www.gutenberg.org/files/15623/15623-h/15623-h.htm.
Richard Dugdale:*The Jukes: A Study of Crime, Pauperism, Disease and Heredity*. http://readingroom.law.gsu.edu/buckvbell/1.

Dr. Ryan Fraser: *What Legacy Are You Leaving for Your Family?* https://eu.jacksonsun.com/story/life/faith/2014/10/10/legacy-leaving-family/17054141/.

Mark Merrill: *A Father's Legacy.* www.markmerrill.com/a-fathers-legacy.

Disciplina: https://www.thefreedictionary.com/Disciplina.

Collins English Dictionary: *Discipline.* www.collinsdictionary.com/dictionary/discipline.

Discere (Latin): www.wordsense.eu/discere.

Corporal punishment in the home: en.wikipedia.org/wiki/Corporal_punishment_in_the_home.

Committee on Psychosocial Aspects of Child and Family Health: *Guidance for effective discipline.* https://pediatrics.aappublications.org/content/101/4/723.short.

Mathilde de Robien: *Do Your Kids Accuse You of Playing Favorites?* https://aleteia.org/2020/01/25/how-to-avoid-the-impression-of-favoritism-in-your-parenting/.

Ryan Chae: *Overprotective Parents and a New Generation of American Children.* https://bpr.berkeley.edu/2019/04/16/overprotective-parents-and-a-new-generation-of-american-children/.

Tracy Trautner: *Overprotective parenting style.* https://www.canr.msu.edu/news/overprotective_parenting_style.

Davon Huss: *Honor Your Father And Mother.* https://www.sermoncentral.com/sermons/honor-your-father-and-mother-davon-huss-sermon-on-commandments-parents-55891.

David Chakranarayan and Ken Ham: *Disciplining Children God's Way.* https://answersingenesis.org/train-up-a-child/christian-parenting/disciplining-children-gods-way/.

Tim Challies: *7 Ways Parents Unfairly Provoke Their Children.* https://www.challies.com/articles/7-ways-parents-unfairly-provoke-our-children/.

Renee Davis: *10 Ways You Might be Exasperating Your Children.* https://www.ibelieve.com/slideshows/10-ways-you-might-be-exasperating-your-children.html.

Kieran Corcoran: *Girl, 13, Commits Suicide by Jumping from Bridge After Her Dad Recorded Video Cutting off Her Hair.* https://www.dailymail.co.uk/news/article-3111907/Girl-13-commits-suicide-jumping-bridge-video-dad-cutting-hair-punishment-posted-online.html.

Kenneth E Hagin: *The Woman Question.* p. 19, 24, 27, and 30. https://irp-cdn.multiscreensite.com/c21a6153/files/uploaded/The_Woman_Question.pdf.

NOTES TO CHAPTER 6

Bill Winston Ministries: *Miracles in the Marketplace.* www.billwinston.org/bwm_productDetail.

Worship Works: *The Ekklesia at Work: Reflections from a Marketplace Minister.* https://worship.works/the-ekklesia-at-work-reflections-from-a-marketplace-minister/.

Chris Patton: *What Is Marketplace Ministry?:* www.christianfaithatwork.com/what-is-marketplace-ministry/.

Os Hillman: *Jesus Was a Workplace Minister.* https://todaygodisfirst.com/jesus-was-a-workplace-minister/.

Avodah (Hebrew עֲבוֹדָה; literally *service*): www.jewishvirtuallibrary.org/avodah.

Ed Silvoso: *Anointed for Business.*

Elizabeth Edwards: https://www.pinterest.com/pin/528187862517555131/.

Albert Einstein: https://www.goodreads.com/quotes/37706-creativity-is-intelligence-having-fun.

Winston Churchill: https://www.quotespedia.org/authors/w/winston-churchill/success-is-walking-from-failure-to-failure-with-no-loss-of-enthusiasm-winston-churchill/.

Ferdinand Nweke: *Marketplace Ministry: Using Your Platform In The Workplace.*

Christ For All Nations: *God Wants Everyone In Full Time Ministry?* https://www.cfan.org.uk/connect/bible-studies/god-wants-everyone-full-time-ministry.

Graham Kendrick: *Give Me This Mountain (Caleb's Song).* https://www.grahamkendrick.co.uk/stories-behind-the-songs/stories-behind-the-song/give-me-this-mountain-caleb-s-song.

NOTES TO CHAPTER 7

Ene I. Ette: *Anoixis Corporation.* http://www.anoixiscorp.com/about/ette-ene.htm.

About the Author

B etty Ivie Nwabineli Msc, PhD, FIBMS, is a published author of two scientific books and a trained business ambassador. She is also a successful entrepreneur, the chief executive officer of her business, *The Best Designer Cakes, Catering, and Training Institute*, based in Newcastle upon Tyne, UK. She was accorded the prestigious award of the *Best Designer Specialist Cake Artist of the Year 2019* by the Society Celebration International Celebrity Organisation. In July 2020, the testimony of her work and faith was featured in the 96th edition of their magazine *Society Celebration International Celebrity Journal*.

Betty Nwabineli is a Marketplace Minister and believes in the Ekklesia as Jesus taught it. She believes that the Ekklesia is the vehicle for transforming nations and that this applies to our whole lives as Christ's followers. She is married to a godly, honourable gentleman (Dr. James Nwabineli) and is a mother and grandmother. She and her husband lead the African Missional Community in Bethshan Church, Washington, UK. God is using them globally to change lives for eternity, equip His saints, and extend His kingdom. Betty says, 'Our goal and prayer as Christian parents should be that our godly children raise godly children who in turn raise godly children'.

Dr. Betty Nwabineli is widely recognised as a Mother in Israel, a motivational speaker, prayer warrior, and team builder and she teaches/ministers the Word of God in the power of the Holy Spirit. She believes that gratitude/thanksgiving to God is the upward call. Nothing will do more to restore contentment and the joy of our salvation than a true spirit of thankfulness.

Betty has led women's groups nationally and internationally. She was the National Women's Coordinator of the Overseas Fellowship of Nigerian Christians (OFNC) of the UK for four consecutive years. She is currently one of the moderators of the global Women's Prayer Altar with over fifty-two thousand members. She is also one of the leaders of the global leadership team of the Kingdom Women in Ministry Globally (KWIMG). She is the leader of the Anointed Praying Mothers (APM) group.

Betty Nwabineli encourages Christians, especially women, to go the extra mile to discover, enhance, and use their God-given talents to God's glory. She strongly believes that to rule is our destiny.

Other Books by the Author

- *A Macro and Micro Study of the Environmental Impacts of Sewage Discharges; A Macro and Micro Study of the Impacts of Sewage Discharges from Marine Outfalls to Aquatic Environments Close to Human Habitats*
- *DVC methods for assessing living bacterial numbers in natural water; Measurement of metabolic activity in bacterial cells by substrate-enhanced INT-reduction and digitised image analysis*

A Heartfelt Tribute to My Wonderful Parents

My parents were blue bloods and of royal lineage. My dad was born in 1918 to Elder Okoh Oboh, who was a centenarian when he died on 23 March 1958, the most senior elder in the whole of my hometown, Ubiaja. An indigene of Idumuso—which is one of the three quarters that make up Eguare, the seat of the Onogie (king) of Ubiaja—he was a very successful and prominent farmer. He was known to be brutally candid and very intelligent, a reasonable measure of which my family members have all inherited, thank God.

My paternal grandmother, Iremete, hailed from Idohalan Quarter, Ubiaja. Her father was an elder and also a chief. He had a hereditary title, 'Oton of Ubiaja', which placed him in the position to oversee the upbringing of the heir-apparent to the throne of Ubiaja.

My mum was born in 1930 to elder and chief Okoyomon Ejie, who was a sawmilling mogul and a very prominent farmer and hunter. He founded the Okoyomon camp in 1915 adjacent Illushi (a village in Edo State in Nigeria), which is three miles square. He hailed from Ebhuru, the second most populated quarter in Ubiaja after Eguare. In the early fifties, he was also a transporter with several Bedford lorries.

My maternal grandmother, Mabane, hailed from the royal family of Ohordua. She was incredibly beautiful, blessed with long hair, and was a trader.

Now to the main characters of my amazing parents: My papa at eight in 1926 enrolled for his primary school education at St Benedict's

Primary School in Oruen, Ubiaja, which has been renamed Oruen Primary School. After eight years of schooling, he graduated in 1934. As a result of his excellent performance at the end-of-school certificate examination, he was employed as a teacher in his alma mater in 1935, where he taught till 1940. He then left for Enugu in the southeast of Nigeria, where he was recruited into the colonial army.

At the end of his military training, he was posted to Durban in South Africa, where he served for six months before he was eventually transferred to Burma (now renamed Myanmar). In Myanmar, he served as a general duties officer. In no time, his British commanding officer noticed his brilliance and intelligence and moved him to the Medical Corp where he started his nursing career. At the end of the Second World War in 1945, my dad returned to Jos (a city in the Middle Belt of Nigeria) after his discharge from the army. He was employed as a nursing orderly at the Jos main hospital. At the completion of his nursing training, he was promoted to the rank of charge nurse.

My parents (Papa and Mama) met in 1947 when he was spending his leave at home in Ubiaja. Since their fathers were bosom friends and co-elders, there was not much ado about protracted courtship. The marriage was packaged within my dad's leave period, at the end of which both of them left for Jos. Their marriage was blessed with nine children (four sons and five daughters). I am the second child and first daughter.

My dad was transferred from Jos to Gusau in 1950, from Gusua to Benin City in 1952, from Benin City to Sapele in 1954, and from Sapele to Auchi in 1962 where their seventh child was born. By mid 1964, my dad was again transferred to Warri in Delta State where their eighth and ninth children were born. Once again, he was transferred to Ossiomo in Edo state where he officially retired as a senior nursing officer. He returned to his hometown with my mum and younger siblings. This was my dad's professional trajectory. Now to my mum's.

My mum was extremely beautiful and hardworking. She was a successful entrepreneur who traded in expensive clothing materials like the Proverbs 31 woman and Lydia in the Book of Acts. She was also a well-trained and incredibly competent seamstress. In her day, she was one of the iconic fashion designers and was famous for her unique sewing skills. I fondly remember my siblings and I excitedly trying on new garments she had made for us to mark an occasion or a celebration. We always turned out pretty, and the greater joy was that we knew she loved making those dresses for us.

Our elder brother recalls how in 1960 she made a profit of £16 during the Christmas and New Year period in her sewing business alone. If you remember that anybody who donated one guinea (one pound and one shilling) was praised to the high heavens at that time, you will realise its value. A new Volkswagen car then was less than £300. Surprisingly, she gave all the money to my dad who took £4 and returned £12 to her.

My mum was kind and an unrelenting sponsor of egalitarianism. Behind all these virtues was a stiff resolve not to entertain indiscipline, something she did to better the lives of her children and mentees. She also ran a confectionery business. You can now begin to guess where my love for cooking and baking comes from.

Our parents' love for self-improvement was insatiable. In the late fifties, our dad used to buy us children's books from Kingsway Stores (one of the leading supermarkets in Nigeria at the time). After dinner most days, he would drill us on the books. His oldest after-dinner student was our mum, who always voluntarily joined and refused to be discouraged no matter how many mistakes she made.

In the late sixties, my dad was taking tuition from Wolsey Hall, Oxford. When we asked whether the course would help to advance his promotion prospect, his reply was, 'No, my children, knowledge is never lost or wasted, rather it will help to expand my intellectual province'.

On his retirement in 1976, he was engaged at the Ubiaja General Hospital as a contract officer. There he helped many patients while some of his colleagues were extorting money from them. Sometimes people still ask our eldest brother, who is now retired and residing in Ubiaja, whether he can be as good as our parents. His retort is usually escapist since our parents are unbeatable.

Playing my memories back: On Sunday mornings, our dad takes over from our mum as the chef. He assembles all his previous days' purchases from Challarams (another leading supermarket in Nigeria in those days) on the dining table. The items will usually range from pork sausages, corned beef, canned mutton, anchor butter, and Brooks tea whose aroma wafts across several metres. Meanwhile, the custom-baked bread would already have been delivered by the baker himself the previous day.

On the same Sunday, in the afternoon, our wonderful mum resumes her role as the family chef to prepare the typical Nigerian tomato sauce with the finest ingredients, special smoked fish, and the choicest parts of boneless beef. With this sauce, we happily eat boiled rice. Our neighbours will be sniffing the aroma from this cuisine.

Writing my parents' eulogy is a tall order for it is difficult to capture in a few sentences. Their full story is a book in itself. May they continue to rest in perpetual peace in our Lord's bosom.

Above: My wonderful parents in their early years. *Below left*: My wonderful mum and I during my first degree (Bachelor of Science in Applied Microbiology) graduation ceremony. My dad and sister in the background. *Below right*: Me and two of my mother's apprentices in the 1950s. She was an iconic fashion designer. She designed and made these outfits including the hat.

Handcrafted bespoke designer celebration cakes by Betty's Best Designer Cakes Company

BETTY
IVIE NWABINELI

'EVERY WOMAN IS A QUEEN IN HER OWN RIGHT.' A TESTIMONY OF HER WORK AND FAITH.

Throughout history, the central role of women in society has ensured the stability, progress and long-term development of nations. One woman in particular, continues to proliferate the role of women today, whilst positioning her impenetrable faith at the forefront of her ideology – 'Taking the Lord Jesus Christ as the author and finisher of one's faith'. Dr Betty Ivie Nwabineli, a devoted Christian and advocate of the Pentecostal persuasion, embraced the Lord in 1969 when she was merely in her third year at the Anglican Girls Grammar School (Ughelli, Delta State, Nigeria). Betty, as she is fondly and commonly called by her peers, is a distinguished medical professional, a creative and prolific writer, a motivational speaker and as aforementioned, a sincere servant of God.

This is a long-overdue testimony, in direct reference to the amazing efforts this magnificent woman has taken to better her community whilst serving the Lord God Almighty every step of the way.

Educational Background:
Betty's aspiration to excel from such an early age gave her the impetus to study Applied Microbiology (Bachelor of Science), from the pioneering University of Benin (Nigeria) in her home country. Following her newly status as a graduate, she enrolled into the compulsory National Youth Service Corps (NYSC) scheme in Kano State, to which she performed remarkably. Due to her strong desires to deepen her knowledge in the medical fields, she proceeded to strengthen her knowledge in the United Kingdom for further studies - she obtained a master's degree in Medical Microbiology and a Doctoral (PhD) in Environmental and Medical Microbiology from the same University of Newcastle. It certainly seems that the medical profession is desirably attractive to the Nwabineli family as Betty's husband was awarded the Gladys Dodds scholarship, to specialise in another area of medicine. However, it was inevitable that with all this profound knowledge Betty would seek a way to divulge and educate other. As a result, using her developed teaching skills garnered from her NYSC scheme, prior to relocating to the UK she taught secondary school students at Iruekpen Gramma School (Iruekpen, Edo State, Nigeria).

Indeed, Betty has numerous specials interests including Clinical/Diagnostic Medical Microbiology, Immunology and Virology, thus fortifying her Fellowship at the Institute of Biomedical Science of the United Kingdom. She's obtained many invaluable experiences at various institutes, occupying various roles; University of Benin Teaching Hospital (Benin), Stobhill Hospital (Glasgow), University of Newcastle (Newcastle), St University Hospital (Dublin) and many more. Nevertheless, Dr Nwabineli's versatility and entrepreneurship enabled her to improve in other areas, allowing incredible personal growth and fantastic opportunities to reveal themselves. She was self-trained in cake-making and decorating, with a qualification from the Wilton Cake Decorating School in the United States of America. This accreditation permitted Betty to start what became a very successful confectionery and catering business in Benin. Her imagination, innovation, and artistic flair led her to design a wide range of divine celebration-cakes. She is very passionate about Homemaking, especially cooking, cake-baking and sugar craft etc. Betty strongly corroborates Margaret Thatcher's renowned quote, "Any woman who understands the problems of running a home will be nearer to understanding the problems of running a country."

Accomplishments Background:
Her skills and experiences as a Doctor of Medical Microbiology, Biomedical Scientist, Cake Artist, Catering and Homemaking, makes her stand out in her business and in the ever-competing world, at large. She passionately and unselfishly shares her skills with people from all walks of life. She also beautifully and powerfully combines her professional skills, business, homemaking (including being a wife and mother) to bear on her care-giving activities in the vineyard of the Lord God.

Dr (Mrs) Ivie Betty Nwabineli's accomplishments does not stop there! Unbeknown to a few, Betty is a gifted and prolific writer. She is an established author, with two scientific books already selling across the globe, and some more in the process of publishing. Her books are growing in popularity and marketed by Amazon and other notable labels across the globe. Her long-awaited book, which will soon hit the shelves is entitled "Fulfilling the Father's Mission".

Another notable mention, Betty was nominated to as a panellist during the Overseas Fellowship of Nigerian Christians (OFNC) annual conference held in August 2018. She was the first to start and lead a Women's group at the Elim Church in Douglas in the Isle of Man. She is a member of OFNC and of the Gideons. Betty later was announced the National Woman's Coordinator for the OFNC of the UK and held her position for a phenomenal four consecutive years.

Family:

Despite her academic prowess and boasting great medical and culinary skills, Betty could not have sustained the rate at which she was developing her career without a loving and nurturing family to keep her health and spirits high. Betty Ivie is married to a wonderful man of God, Dr Nwachukwu James Nwabineli, (a senior consultant of Obstetrics and Gynaecology), who is supportive and 'a truest friend'. According to Betty, her husband is always the 'man after her heart', still, after over forty-one years of a blissful marriage and counting! For years, she used her late mother as the ideal role model, but what has also kept her motivation intact is her love for God and unwavering faith. She asserts that Proverbs 31 is her living creed. Betty understands she is far from perfect, but through following this Proverb, fearing God and allowing the Holy Spirit to work within her, she continues to take momentous steps towards becoming a godly woman. Betty and James, her husband, are seniors in their Church (The Bethshan Church, Washington, Tyne and Wear) and leaders of the African Missionary Community in their church. They are blessed with grown up children, who

were thoroughly-brought-up in the ways of the Lord God and all their children are doing extremely well in their chosen careers. Their married life and parenting of their children in the ways of the Lord God has drawn attraction from various families, hence a lot of others take after them and adapt to their Christian-like household. It is unsurprising to note; the

couple have been involved in conducting marriage seminars and conferences in the UK and Nigeria.

They were recently featured in the book titled "The Beauty of Relationships – Focus on Marriage" by Dr Ikechukwu Medumere. Part of the vision of the Nwabineli's is to empower married couples and those wishing to get married with adequate resources and knowledge to make the best of their married lives. They truly are an amazing couple, other acts of their kindness can be seen here after involving themselves with a ministry in Kenya that buys off sex slaves from their captors, settle them in the church, rehabilitate them and empower them to find their solace and sustenance in the Lord God.

Scope and Benefits of her work:
Betty Nwabineli is an 'Anointed Marketplace Minister' – meaning that she purposely takes her Christian faith and inculcates God's work into her career and business curricula, as if she works as a fulltime gospel minister. Into the Lord's vineyard she does the work of an Evangelist. She teaches and encourages people who are called by God to serve. Betty urges Christians in the marketplace to come to the spiritual realization; that workplace and business are practical vehicles to turn lives around to God. And that no matter what one is engaged in, being a medical doctor, lawyer, teacher, entrepreneur, farmer, administrator, nurse etc. – 'We are ambassadors for the kingdom of God'. Betty is long-established member of the Kingdom Women in Ministry

Globally (KWIMG). The vision of KWIMG is to receive and release the Word of God and Sound to nations, where it operates on three frequencies: Leadership, Collaboration and Missions. KWIMG organises local and international missions, just as it trains and mentors Kingdom Women for effectiveness. It entails team work, with specific assignments to chosen territories where the less privileged are empowered through men and women, to empower others. The bottom line of the activities is ministration through preaching and teaching of the gospel and to raise disciples, in the end times.

Life's Philosophy:
Betty believes that family is what empowers us to achieve anything. Being a loving wife to her husband; dutiful and caring Mother to her Children; Giver of Medicare to the sick (God then heals) and Vending of hope. She is very grateful for the abundant talents and gifts God has blessed her with, in addition to the virtues she continues to carry and exhibit from her late mother. One virtue in particular is, her altruistic need to invest in people. We are not merely referring to investment as the influx of financial resources, no. It is very possible to invest money in someone and yet not care about the person. Betty invokes her time, love, and generosity to the aid of many. She has touched countless hearts, and everyone she has encountered, can testify to her altruism. But Betty gives all the glory to God and Him alone. She encourages everyone else, especially women to go the extra mile to discover, enhance and use their God-given talents to God's glory. Betty is very passionate about empowering women and equipping them with the necessary tools to flourish in today's society, because echoing our opening passage, throughout history, the central role of women in society has ensured the stability, progress and long-term development of nations.

The Best Designer

Cakes,

Catering And

Training Institute.

Newcastle Upon Tyne

United Kingdom

The testimony of my faith and work published in the *International Society Celebrity Journal* (July 2020)

Printed in Great Britain
by Amazon

59875454R00142